Off-Leash Dog Play

A Complete Guide
to Safety and Fun

Robin Bennett, CPDT
Susan Briggs, CKO

C&R Publishing, LLC ~ Woodbridge, Virginia

A Division of Dream Dog Productions, LLC

Off-Leash Dog Play
A Complete Guide to Safety and Fun
By Robin Bennett, CPDT, and Susan Briggs, CKO

Published by:
C&R Publishing, a division of
Dream Dog Productions, LLC
P.O. Box 4227
Woodbridge VA 22194-4227 USA
www.dreamdogproductions.com

Bennett, Robin and Briggs, Susan
Off-Leash Dog Play
Robin Bennett, CPDT
Susan Briggs, CKO
P.cm.
Includes index
ISBN 978-1-933562-20-9
1. Pets 2. Dogs

Cover by Susan Glasgow, http://www.glasgowgraphics.com
Front Cover Labrador Retriever photo, "Nilla" by Vicki Gotchcr

All other photos courtesy of the author with the following exceptions:
Pam Nashman (rottweiler on p. 39,); Martha Greene (p. 62); Eileen Fulk (left photo on p. 66 and 3rd photo from top on p. 97); Heather Staas (p. 103); Debbie Oliver (p. 109); Martha Walker (top photo on p. 120); Diana Craig (bottom photo on p. 120); Julie Fudge Smith (left photo on p. 121)

10   9   8   7   6   5   4   3   2

Acknowledgements

ROBIN: There are so many people involved in writing a book that to try to name each of them would take up an entire book itself.

First and foremost, to my husband, Greg. You have immeasurable patience for my pursuit of all things dog-related. Thank you for allowing me time to pursue my passion. To my children, Leanna and Nathan. You're more wonderful with each day. Thank you for all your support. I love you all very much.

To Colleen Pelar, my friend and business partner extraordinaire. Without you none of this would have ever made it to print. Thank you for taking a bunch of "stuff," poring over it (and adding a bunch of commas), and turning it into a book.

To Susan, my co-author. Thanks for your inspiration in getting this book underway and your willingness to take on the project together. You're a huge asset to ABKA and the daycare industry.

To the tremendous staff at All About Dogs: Keely Bovais, Diana Craig, Annmarie Dykes, Roz Ferber, Eileen Fulk, Vicki Gotcher, Mary Graham, Chris Johnson, Kim Kamphaus, Pam Nashman, Colleen Pelar, Vicky Shields-Harding, and Martha Walker. Your thought-provoking questions and discussions about dog behavior helped form some of the thoughts in this book. I am thankful to have you as friends and co-workers. I have yet to see a better team!

Finally, thanks be to God. For Your grace, love, forgiveness, and blessings. I owe a great deal of gratitude to my friends at Ebenezer United Methodist Church, Stafford, Virginia. You help keep my feet on the ground and my eyes on God. For Pastor Mark A. Miller, Nancy Buechler, and Virginia Richardson, thank you for holding me accountable to life's true priorities.

Robin K. Bennett
www.allaboutdogdaycare.com
www.allaboutdogsinc.com

SUSAN: As a first-time author, you quickly learn that writing a book is a team effort. The writing process draws from many experiences in your life, some unrelated to the book subject. Hallie, my smooth collie, inspired my career shift to the pet industry. My dream job would let me take her to work with me. When the opportunity came to exit the corporate world, I found two of the best business partners available in Frances Armstrong and Crista Meyer. Our partnership success is attributed to our shared passion for each dog's wellbeing and our uncompromising focus on pet health and safety in the operation of Urban Tails. Frances and Crista are great supporters of my many "ideas" and worked with Penni Phillips and Caley Eichenlaub to ensure Urban Tails continued to operate successfully as I spent time writing this book.

In 2000, we brought our vision of pet care to ABKA, the trade association for pet care professionals, and with naïve enthusiasm talked about the great benefits of dog daycare and cage-free boarding. We did not realize that these services were not fully embraced by the association at the time. Fortunately, Region 8 was comprised of open-minded and welcoming members who actually encouraged us to provide information on these services. Without the support from Al & Suzanne Locker, Charlotte Biggs, and Betty Gayle, this book would never have been envisioned. Jim Krack and Bob Payne were very receptive to including dog daycare services into the association and this led to my service as Dog Daycare Section chair.

A priority goal as chair was to develop the first set of industry operating standards. The operating standards were created with the help of a dedicated group of daycare owners from the Dog Daycare Yahoo group list. This group of owners openly shared information and taught me key aspects of managing dog behavior for a fun and safe daycare experience. It is interesting how you gain professional respect and relationships through a group forum without actually meeting. Through the years the following individuals have shared invaluable information that in many ways is contained in this book: Heather Staas, Cristal Newell, Janet Galante, Marilyn Marks, Tommy Fleming, Susan Ferry, and Laurie Zurborg.

It was through this group that I also met Robin, my co-author. During an ABKA seminar, she inspired me to relook at our own daycare operations when she pointed out that emotional health of dogs is just as important as their physical safety.

Having responsibility for training our staff at Urban Tails actually drove this project due to the frustration of not finding a comprehensive resource for teaching the basics of dog language. Nancy Parsley and PJ Yruegaz served as great guinea pigs to my early training programs and as the "real-world" confirmation for content in this book. Their honest input and feedback served as my reality check that this would work as a training guide.

Taking time away from their own businesses to provide feedback on the content of this book were Debbie Oliver and Jim Burwell. Their input was an important validation from industry peers that this resource was headed in the right direction. Their edits and content additions result in a better final product. Colleen Pelar and Robin have been great leaders in the technical aspect of book writing and publishing, and I appreciate their patience and guidance.

Finally, but probably most important, is the encouragement and support from my family. Throughout my life my parents, Gary & Adrianna Briggs, instilled in me the confidence to pursue whatever dream I had. My father's entrepreneurial spirit was passed on and helped bring the dream of Urban Tails to a reality. Bill Kamps has provided emotional, businesss, and financial support as I pursued my pet industry career dreams. He selected our second canine family member, Hank, a fun-loving golden retriever and let me keep Sheppy, the mix breed I found on the street one Saturday afternoon. From each of these kids and the many dogs that visit Urban Tails, they connected my research to realities of dog life in an off-leash group setting.

All of these people provided positive and encouraging support to my dreams and ideas. I am thankful to each one and encourage you  to not only share your knowledge, but also create a positive environment to inspire others to follow a dream.

~ Susan Briggs
www.urbantails.cc

A Letter to our Readers

The recent popularity of dog social activities in the form of dog parks, dog daycares, social play dates, and playgroup sessions requires that humans learn how to "speak dog." There is a renewed interest and recognized need for this information among pet professionals. Many different resources are available on dog language, but nothing specifically targets the many needs of off-leash playgroup managers in understanding the communication that occurs when a group of dogs is playing off leash together.

Off-leash Dog Play was written as a resource for pet professionals. Whether you operate or work in a dog daycare, a pet boarding facility, a kennel, or a shelter, or you offer off-leash playgroups in another setting, we want you to have safe and fun playtimes. Mistakes can result in serious injuries or even death to the dogs in your care. We think you can avoid these mistakes. We share a passion for the safety of dogs who participate in group play activities. Our goal in writing this book is to help ensure both the physical health and the emotional well-being of all dogs who participate in off-leash playgroups. Overseeing dogs playing off-leash is an incredible adventure and a great deal of responsibility. Remember to keep the dogs safe.

~ Robin Bennett
~ Susan Briggs

Table of Contents

Chapter 1 –
Dog Language Basics

Dogs are social animals. By and large, they enjoy the company of people and other dogs. Many enjoy off-leash dog play. Today's dog owners can easily find social activities for their dogs at dog parks, doggy daycares, social play dates and playtime activities during boarding. Social playgroups meet an instinctual need for many dogs.

Dogs use a very effective language to communicate within their groups. A well-socialized dog learns this language as a puppy. Dog language helps dogs conserve energy, ensure survival and live together peacefully as a pack. Dogs communicate with body postures, facial expressions, and vocalizations. Much of their language is subtle and occurs extremely fast to our human eyes. Humans and dogs have miscommunications every day. To avoid these miscommunications, we need to learn how to understand dog language.

Animals living in social groups require language to avoid disputes and to live peacefully together. Language is the fundamental tool used by dogs to:

- Identify individuals
- Maintain social affiliations
- Reduce competition

Dogs view the world as things that are either familiar or unfamiliar. Their family group, home territory, and neighborhood are examples of familiar things. Dogs living with the familiar feel safe. They stay in a calm state, and their posture is relaxed. When they sense something unfamiliar, dogs move from being relaxed to alert. Canine body language developed so dogs could quickly identify the unfamiliar and determine the risk of danger to themselves and others.

Dogs are always communicating their emotional state or mood through their posture. Dog language also includes deliberate signals of intent, such as friendly greetings, possessive warnings, rank order status, etc.

Dogs use multiple senses to communicate. Their highly developed sense of smell is used to communicate up close and over a long range. Visual body language is used over close and medium distances. Vocal tools are used for close and long-range communication.

We can learn to read and understand dog language. The better your ability in this area, the safer your playgroup session will be. In off-leash playgroups, it is important to recognize, differentiate, and understand dog language expressions. These include signals of social rank, indications of concern, and warnings of physical attack. Throughout this chapter we will classify signals using an off-leash play management traffic signal.

The goal is to have mostly green-light behavior during off-leash play. This is possible with a well-screened and well-managed group of dogs. However, yellow cautions will occasionally occur even in the best-managed groups. This chapter will help you recognize them and intervene early. By responding to yellow caution signals, you will be managing proactively. As a result, the more serious red signals will rarely be seen.

Mgmt Signal	Meaning
Green	Green—Positive off-leash play. Let play and interactions proceed.
Yellow	Yellow—Concern for miscommunication or conflict in off-leash play. Monitor interactions with caution. Watch for signs of stress, fear, alert, or other warning signals. May require action to intervene and redirect behaviors.
Red	Red—High risk in off-leash play, intervene to stop action. Risk of conflict is increased due to high arousal, extreme stress, or fear

SCENT COMMUNICATION

Smell is the most highly developed sense in dogs. It is hundreds of times more sensitive than our own sense of smell. The section of the dog's brain that processes scent signals is larger in size and complexity than ours. Dogs have an organ that helps them detect pheromones or body chemical scents, which help them quickly identify familiar animals and people.

Scientific testing has confirmed that intact male dogs smell "male." Neutering changes a dog's odor. Odor affects canine interactions, and scent is often the first sense dogs use in their communication.

Sniffing interrupts a dog's normal breathing pattern to provide the dog with information. In one sniff during a greeting, the dog will determine:

- Are you familiar?
- Where are you from?
- How are you?
- What is your age?
- What is your sex?
- What is your emotional state?

During dog-to-dog greetings, we observe dogs sniffing in a common pattern. The mouth and neck areas are sniffed first, followed by sniffing of the rear end and genital area. Dogs spend a lot of time sniffing the genitals and rear. This is an important part of dog communication, and we need to allow time for it.

Scent that lingers from urine and feces serves as long-distance communication to other dogs. Many male dogs urinate high so that others will smell their mark more easily. By sniffing eliminations dogs find out about their world:

- Who is in the area
- How long ago they were there
- Sex and breeding status of animals in the area
- Health of other dogs
- Age of other dogs

Although we cannot decipher these scent messages, we need to recognize that they are important in dog communication. A well-managed playgroup allows dogs to smell each other in greeting rituals. Entryways and enclosures should be designed to provide safe scent communication. Allow sniffing greetings until all dogs are comfortable with the new dog joining the group. For more information on dog greetings, see chapter 6.

VISUAL COMMUNICATION

Dogs are more likely to respond to signals they see than those they hear. Dogs read visual signals very quickly and respond instantly with their own body language signals. Keep in mind the importance of visual communication as you manage off-leash playgroups. Your body movements will be more effective than your voice or words. Good dog leaders communicate very effectively without saying a single word.

Visual body signals are detailed later in this chapter. Before we focus on them, we will review the vocal signals.

VOCAL COMMUNICATION

Vocal signals are a sort of backup to the body language signals. You can recognize a wide range of vocalizations from a single dog. Each vocalization has a different sound and meaning. An alarm bark signaling the approach of a stranger differs in tone, pace, and repetition from an excited play bark.

- **Barking** is the most common vocal signal and is used as an alarm, greeting, attention-seeking, or warning to stay away. These barks will vary and you can learn to recognize the differences in each one.
  - o Low pitch means confidence or threatening
  - o High pitch indicates fear, stress, or insecurity
  - o Faster pace reflects more arousal and excitement
- **Growling** is a warning signal.
  - o Low pitch means confidence or threatening
  - o High pitch indicates fear or insecurity
  - o Frequent changes in pitch and steadiness indicate an unsure dog
- **Howling** is a long-distance signal. Dogs tend to howl when lonely.
- **Whining** is a long high-pitched sound associated with distress, insecurity, or fear. It is a normal sound

for puppies who are alone or frustrated trying to solve a problem. It can also be an attention-seeking signal.

- **Whimpering** is a soft sound indicating fear or submission.
- **Yelping** sounds like a short high-pitch bark and is generally in response to sudden and unexpected pain.
- **Screaming** is a high-pitched prolonged yelp that signals pain or panic from a dog.
- **Champing** is a noisy chewing motion (when there is nothing to chew) that indicates friendliness, insecurity, or submission. This is one of the first sounds puppies hear when their siblings nurse so it can sometimes be a sound associated with satisfaction.

Common sounds heard during off-leash playgroups are listed in the table by management traffic signal along with probable related dog emotions and meanings.

Mgmt Signal	Sound	Dog Emotion	Meaning
Green	Short bark, "ruff"	Hello, let's play	Pleasure & excitement
	Bark rising in pitch	This is fun	Enjoyable play
	Howl	I hear you	Group howl
	Champing	I'm satisfied	Friendly & no threat
	Growl (soft & playful)	I want to play	Playful & excited
	Whine	I want	Excited & eager
Yellow	Rapid barking	Calling the pack	Alert call or alarm bark
	High-pitch barking	Help, I don't like this	Stress signal
	Single sharp bark	Stop! What's that?	Alert
	Soft, short growl	Stop!	Warning
	Whine (low)	What's that?	Alert
	Moaning bark	I'm not sure about this	Anxious
Red	Long, deep, low growl	Back off! Beware!	Annoyed & confident
	Growl-bark	I'm upset & frightened	Fearful & annoyed. May fight if pushed
	Long growl w/ pitch changes	I'm terrified!	Extreme fear in more submissive dog
	Whine	I need	Distress or fear
	Whimper	I'm hurt or scared	Stress
	Yelp	I'm hurt & scared	Injured, physically or emotionally
	Scream	Help, help! I'm very scared!	Extreme fear. Sound can trigger prey drive in other dogs

BODY LANGUAGE

Dogs communicate using their entire bodies from head to tail. This means there are quite a few signals being sent at once, and it can be difficult for us to read them as quickly as they are being sent. With practice, we can improve the speed with which we identify and interpret these signals and learn how to communicate back in short conversations.

Body language signals are sent through the dogs'

- Body posture
- Ears
- Tails
- Facial expressions

The best place to start learning and reading dog body language is to focus on body posture. From there you can move to the details of ears, tails, and facial expressions. You may be confused when mixed signals are sent from different body parts. Although it is initially helpful to learn by focusing on each body part, your goal is to focus on the full picture of signals. Reading only one part of the dog's body can be like taking a quotation out of context.

Postures and Movement

Body posture and movement signal a dog's motivation or intent. Weight and balance are magnified in the dog's mind. Dogs are very sensitive to subtle weight shifts forward and backward. They also notice changes in body tension and breathing patterns. These subtle signs have a great deal of meaning in dog language, but they are not always obvious to the untrained human eye.

Body posture is easiest to describe by comparing neutral, relaxed posture with the two extremes of confidence and fear. Keep in mind that you rarely see the two extremes, especially in off-leash playgroups. You will see dogs all along the continuum. Watch the dogs' posture. Are they showing confidence? Comfort? Low rank? Fear?

- Neutral & Relaxed Body Posture
  - Balanced on all four legs
  - Lacks tension
  - Movement is relaxed, loose, and curvy
- Confident Body Posture
  - Tall and weight forward on front legs
  - Dog appears large
  - Stiff legs
  - Body movement tends to be stiff and tense
- Fearful or Subordinate Body Posture
  - Low (near ground) and weight shifted backward toward rear
  - Dog appears small
  - Legs crouched
  - Body movement tends to be tense and slow

Balanced Posture

Confident Posture

Fearful Posture

Ears

Dogs can communicate through the position and movement of their ears. Keep in mind the breed-type and natural ear carriage when evaluating ear signals. For instance, dogs with cropped ears may send out unintentional alert signals. This can sometimes lead to miscommunication with other dogs. Common ear positions and their potential meanings are:

- Neutral position (dependent on natural breed carriage)
  - Muscles loose
  - Relaxed state
- Forward (from neutral position)
  - Alert
  - Confident
  - Attentive
  - Interested
  - Aggressive
- Backward (from neutral position)
  - Subordinate
  - Insecure
  - Friendly
- Flattened (backward and against head)
  - Fearful
- Spread sideways (from neutral position)
  - Anxious
  - Unsure

To clearly understand their meaning, ear signals must be considered in combination with other body signals. The table outlines common ear positions, dog's emotion, and their common meanings sorted by off-leash management traffic signal.

Mgmt Signal	Ear Position	Dog Emotion	Meaning
Green	Neutral	I'm at ease	Relaxed
	Erect	What's that?	Attentive, Interest
	Backward	I'm no threat	Friendly, Submissive
Yellow	Forward	I'm in charge	Confident, Interest
	Flattened	I'm scared	Threatened, Fearful
	Spread Sideways	I'm not sure	Anxious, Unsure

Neutral Ears, Relaxed

Erect Ears, Attentive

Erect Ears, Attentive

Flattened Ears, Scared

Forward Ears, Confident

Forward Ears, Confident

Backward Ears, Submissive

Sideways Ears, Unsure

Erect Ears, Interest

Sideways Ears, Unsure

Neutral Ears, Relaxed

Forward Ears, Interest

Tails

As with ears, consider the natural tail carriage and breed-type of the dog when considering tail communications. Some dogs have a naturally high or low tail carriage, even when relaxed. Evaluate the tail signal in combination with those of the body posture and facial expression.

- Neutral
  - o Dependent on natural breed carriage
  - o Lower than horizontal position
  - o Muscles loose
  - o Relaxed state
- High
  - o Horizontal or higher carriage (higher over back indicates more confidence and excitement)
  - o Confidence
- Low
  - o Subordinate or less confident (lower to between legs indicates less confidence or increased fear)
  - o Discomfort
  - o Insecurity
  - o Fear

Consider the movement or wag of the tail when you evaluate its signals. The speed indicates the level of arousal or excitement. Generally speaking, a faster tail wag indicates more excitement. Although this could be happy excitement when seeing an owner, it might also be nervous excitement from seeing a threatening stranger. It's important to consider all the signals together when trying to read the dog.

The table below outlines common tail positions, the dog's emotions, and their common meanings sorted by off-leash management traffic signal.

Mgmt Signal	Tail Position Or Movement	Dog Emotion	Meaning
Green	Neutral position	I'm at ease	Relaxed
	Large wags at moderate speed; may be in circles	I like you	Friendly, happy
	Small wags at moderate speed	Hello	Friendly greeting
	Wags at slow speed	I like that I don't under-stand	Pleased Problem solving
Yellow	High position	I'm in charge	Confident
	Low position	I'm no threat	Subordinate (less confident)
	Fast small wags	I'm interested	Excitement
Red	Slow & small rhythmic wags	I'm watching with concern	On guard

Neutral, relaxed tail position

Tail rises with increase in confidence

Base of tail higher than spine

Most confident

Neutral, relaxed tail position

Tail *lowers with decrease in confidence*

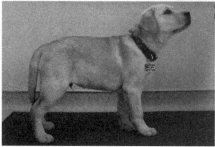

Base of tail lower than spine

Least confident

FACIAL EXPRESSIONS

A dog's facial expression completes the picture of signals started by the body posture, ears, and tail. By observing facial tension, eyes, mouth, and teeth, you can identify the dog's motivation. Black dogs and dogs with darker faces are harder to read in this area. This may be the reason why many dogs seem more nervous of black dogs; their communication signals are harder to read. Some breed-types have distinct facial markings that aid in the interpretation of their signals. For instance, rottweilers and many tricolor dogs have brown spots on their eyebrows that make their eyes more visible.

When observing facial expressions begin by looking for signs of tension in the muscles around the muzzle and forehead. In a neutral expression, the muscles are loose and relaxed. When tense the dog will have visible and pronounced wrinkles around the mouth and in the forehead. Observe key parts of the face for specific meanings of the expressions.

- Eyes
    - Soft eyes (small pupils) describe the neutral relaxed state
    - Larger pupil size indicates higher level of arousal
    - Hard eyes and dilated pupils may indicate high confidence. This can be a threatening signal
    - Half-moon eye occurs when whites of the eye are visible and indicates a fearful state (more white than normal eye position)
    - Smaller and elongated eyes indicate a passive and less confident signal
- Mouth
    - Relaxed and slightly open is the neutral relaxed state
    - Closed mouth signals attention or interest

- o Open with lips pursed forward (into a "C" shape) signals annoyance in a highly confident dog
- o Open with lips pulled back signals threat in a fearful dog
- o More exposure of teeth and gums, the greater the signaled threat

The table below outlines common facial expressions, dog's emotions, and their common meanings sorted by off-leash management traffic signal.

Mgmt Signal	Facial Expression	Dog Emotion	Meaning
Green	Relaxed muzzle & forehead	I'm happy	Relaxed
	Soft eyes	I'm happy	Relaxed
	Blinking eyes	I'm no threat	Friendly, less confident
	Look away; avoids eye contact	I'm no threat	Less confident, lower in rank
	Mouth slightly opened or softly closed	I'm happy	Relaxed
Yellow	Slight wrinkling of muzzle & forehead	I'm concerned	Alert
	Narrow elongated eyes	I'm no threat	Less confident, lower in rank
	Mouth pursed forward in "C" shape & mostly closed	Go away	Annoyed; confident dog
	Lips drawn back & mostly closed	Go away	Annoyed; subordinate dog
	Mouth wide open, lips drawn back with panting	I'm afraid. I'm in pain	Fear in a less confident dog Stress signal
	Dilated Pupils	I'm nervous or excited	Arousal, stress
Red	Hard eyes with direct staring	I challenge you. Stop that!	Threat signal
	Half-moon eyes	I'm scared	Threat signal
	Mouth pursed forward in "C" shape & showing a lot of teeth	Go away	Warning; confident dog
	Lips drawn back & showing a lot of teeth	Go away	Warning; fearful dog
	Mouth closed tight with tension	I challenge you. Stop that!	Threat signal

Soft eyes, relaxed muzzle *Dilated pupils, half-moon eye*

Hard eyes, direct stare *Half-moon eye*

Elongated eye *Narrowed eyes*

Relaxed, open mouth

Muzzle closed, wrinkled brow

Mouth pursed in "C" shape

Lips drawn, mouth closed

Lips drawn, mouth open

Lips drawn, teeth showing

EMOTIONAL STATES

Like us, our dogs experience a wide range of emotions during their daily life. By reading dog body language, you can quickly assess the current emotional state of a dog. This is an important skill in managing off-leash playgroups to ensure that play is fun for everyone. Dogs who are bullied or overwhelmed in off-leash playgroups lose self-confidence and emotional well-being. This can require long-term behavior rehabilitation that could have easily been prevented.

Appendix A includes three charts of dog emotions organized by the management traffic signals. The charts list emotional states including the common body posture, movement, ear position, tail carriage, facial expression, and vocalization of each. Photo pages are also included as a visual snapshot of some of the more common emotional states observed. These charts translate the snapshot picture of body language into an emotional state. These are good tools to improve your fluency in dog language.

Chapter 2 –
Social Interactions

In dog-to-dog social interactions, body language signals form expressions that create conversations. These expressions become common behaviors that are understood by dogs. Is all behavior communication? When an animal does something that causes another animal to change his behavior, communication is occurring. For example, if you cough while seated in a movie theater and the person next to you gets up and changes seats, your cough was a form of communication.

In off-leash playgroups, understanding canine social interactions ensures you can manage the harmony and stability within the group. Any change to the group by adding or removing a dog will trigger new interactions. Dogs who read and respond appropriately to other dogs' signals are generally better in off-leash play sessions than those that do not. This should be one of the determining factors when screening dogs for their appropriateness in an off-leash playgroup.

How well dogs converse and interact with each other depends on their social history. Dogs with good communication skills often had numerous positive encounters with a wide range of different dogs during puppyhood. Dogs who had either very few or bad experiences with other dogs when they were puppies are often poor communicators. They do not read the subtle signals of other dogs and find it difficult to send the proper signals themselves. This miscommunication can result in conflict. Well-socialized dogs easily diffuse conflict and rarely get into fights.

SOCIAL BEHAVIORS

Dog behaviors can be categorized into several behavior types:

- Ritualized behaviors
- Infantile behaviors
- Appeasement behaviors
- Confidence behaviors
- Displacement behaviors
- Correcting behaviors
- Warning behaviors

Ritualized behaviors are common behaviors used to gain cooperation. For example, the common greeting pattern in which one dog sniffs another dog's mouth and neck followed by the rear and genitals is a ritualized behavior. Ritualized behaviors ensure safety by turning off threats and inhibiting aggression.

The domesticated adult dog behaves in a more juvenile manner than the adult wolf. As a result, many of the behaviors commonly observed in puppies are modified and used in social conversations among adult dogs. These are referred to as *infantile behaviors* and are often used as *appeasement gestures*. Appeasement gestures are active displays of deference and show respect to another dog. These behaviors are used to avoid conflicts and confrontations. Since they serve to pacify the other dog these behaviors are also called *pacifying gestures*. A dog who blinks when approached by another dog is displaying an appeasement gesture. Posturing in a side roll or turn is an example of a pacifying gesture.

Gestures that reinforce the higher rank of a particular dog are referred to as *confidence behaviors*. These gestures send messages regarding rank and help to establish hierarchies while, at the same time, avoid actual serious conflicts. An appeasement or pacifying gesture in response to a confidence behavior will confirm the status of each dog. Conflict can occur in situations where the receiving dog chooses to challenge the confident gesture rather than respond with appeasement. This conflict may be a brief squabble or it may result in a fight.

Normal behavior shown at an inappropriate time and appearing out of context for the occasion is called *displacement behavior*. For instance, a dog suddenly needs to scratch his neck while another dog is sniffing him.

Educating puppies is one of the most important tasks for the mother dog. A good dog mother is patient and attentive, but will use *correcting behavior* if her puppy is not well-mannered. These maternal corrections help the puppy learn good social skills and appropriate dog language. The mother will growl and use correcting behaviors without harming the puppy. Adult dogs use correcting behaviors when another dog displays rude or inappropriate behaviors. Appropriate corrections are a part of dog conversations. To lead off-leash playgroups, you need to understand and allow appropriate dog-to-dog corrections.

Warning behaviors generally relate to space. An individual dog's need for personal space will vary. In addition, the context and stress levels of a situation affect a dog's sensitivity to space. Managing off-leash playgroups requires you to recognize and eliminate pushy and rude space-invading behaviors from dogs. Initial warning looks happen very quickly and can be very subtle. It is also important to recognize and eliminate guarding behaviors. Playgroup leaders should intervene before there is a reactive or aggressive response to these warnings.

SOCIAL GESTURES

Dog conversations are made up of various gestures displayed between two or more dogs during social interactions. The type of response from the receiving dog is just as important as the display from the sending dog. In our own conversations, one person may take a joke in fun while another person is offended. You watch for a response from the audience to determine the appropriateness of a joke or conversation. This is also true in dog conversations. Observing reactions is important confirmation that each dog is enjoying the social interactions and play. Your responsibility in managing off-leash playgroups is to ensure not only the physical, but also the emotional health of each dog.

Following is a listing, in alphabetical order, of common dog-to-dog social gestures.

- **Back Roll**–dog rolls on back and rubs shoulders on the ground. Often occurs after something pleasant.
- **Blinking**–dog is showing friendliness or submission when he blinks at another dog. A higher-ranking dog may blink to show acceptance of a subordinate's greeting.
- **Champing**–shows friendliness towards a dog.
- **Freezing**–no movement with tension and stiff body posture. A warning signal of imminent threat.
- **Guarding**–nose is pointed away and eyes looking at the other dog. Signal is used to establish ownership or possession of something (e.g., toy, water bowl, physical space, human, etc). There will be tension in the facial expression that confirms the warning signal.
- **Licking**–face licking is often a submissive gesture.
- **Lip Licking** - quick flick of tongue out of mouth. Signal of discomfort or uneasiness.
- **Look Away**–avoidance of direct eye contact with another dog. Polite and friendly gesture from a subordinate to a higher-ranking dog. Generally seen in friendly neutral social groups (exception is during play or conflict when friendly dogs do make eye contact). When accompanied by stress signals, it is a signal of discomfort and avoidance.

- **Mounting**–a social behavior that has a wide variety of meanings. It can be a sign of confidence or play as well as the behavior of a nervous or agitated dog. Both males and females exhibit mounting behavior.
- **Muzzle Nudge**–one dog gently nudges another on the muzzle with his own. Normally the subordinate dog nudges a higher-ranking dog. It shows friendliness and acceptance. Sometimes dogs will poke the side of another dog's throat as a display of confidence.
- **Muzzle Grasp**–commonly seen in a mother dog educating her puppies. She grabs them around the muzzle or head with her mouth as a form of correction. The puppies learn to show passive submission. With two adult dogs, the muzzle grasp is used in play and mild conflicts; it is not typically used in serious fights.
- **Pawing**–touching an animal or object with a paw is an attention-getting signal. A paw on another dog's back is a confidence signal. Pawing can also be used as a signal without physical touch, called a paw lift. Used by a subordinate dog to a higher-ranking one in greeting or as a pacifying gesture. The paw lift may also be observed when a dog is curious, feels anticipation, or is stalking.
- **Piloerection (Raised Hackles)**–hair bristles and stands erect signaling excitement. The meaning can range from general excitement to fear and insecurity to confidence and threat.
- **Scratching**–This is sometimes a displacement behavior. It can be a signal that the dog is uncomfortable with the proximity of another dog.
- **Shake-off**–dog shakes his body as if his fur is wet even when he's dry. Non-threatening signal often observed after an uncomfortable event.
- **Shoulder Bump**–higher-ranking dog uses his shoulder to bump a subordinate dog. This is a signal to

move out of the path of more confident dog. Leaning on another dog is a subtle form of this signal; acceptance is shown when the other dog moves. This is also sometimes used to initiate play.

- **Side Roll**–dog rolls on side or back and breaks off eye contact. Usually signals inferior status.
- **Side Turn**–subordinate dog turns his side or rear toward a higher-ranking dog. A confident dog who turns his side signals a slightly lower social rank. When hindquarters are turned, there is generally a greater social gap.
- **Snarl**–dog draws back his lips and shows his teeth. Confident dogs snarl with lips curled forward in a "C" shape.
- **Stand Over**–a dog stands with his muzzle and head over shoulders of another dog. May also take the form of standing over a dog lying on the ground. Signal of higher rank that may or may not be accepted. Often seen during play.
- **Standing Still**–standing still with a relaxed body posture is a signal sent by a confident dog to calm a nervous subordinate.
- **Staring**–making direct eye contact with another dog or object. Signals interest, curiosity, alerting, guarding, targeting, predation, or direct threat. Observe other body language to determine motivation.
- **Twist Movement**–sitting dog twists one leg out to the side. The signal pacifies the other dog. Originated when mother overturns puppies by placing her nose against their groins.
- **Yawn**–when the dog is not tired, this is a friendly or stress signal. A higher-ranking dog yawns to show friendliness to the subordinate and vice versa. A dog may yawn when uncomfortable and feels stressed in a situation. The yawn is often the first signal that a dog is uneasy.

The following page contains a table of common social gestures sorted by our management traffic signal.

It is important to focus on the receiving dog's response to these social signals. The yellow signals are an important part of dog conversations and, when appropriate, should be allowed during off-leash playgroups. Dogs need to be able to communicate. If we correct them for giving warning signals, they may just stop giving them. If that happens, they lose a vital part of their communication process and may skip the warning and go straight to conflict. For instance, an adult dog who growls when a rowdy youngster charges into him with a shoulder bump is providing an appropriate correction for rude behavior.

Consider the appropriateness of the warning to the context of the offense and situation. A dog who snarls and snaps when another dog walks within 2-3 feet of him shows an extreme sensitivity of his personal space. While we should still let the dog snarl, we should also take steps to increase that dog's space tolerance or ensure he is in a playgroup with fewer dogs. By understanding dog social signals, you learn how to respond as a leader for the well-being of all dogs in the playgroup.

For more information on the uses of these signals, see the separate chapters on play, stress, and aggression.

Mgmt Signal	Social Gesture
Green	Back roll
	Blinking
	Champing
	Licking
	Look away
	Mounting - during play
	Muzzle nudge
	Pawing – paw lift during greeting
	Pawing – paw lift when curious
	Piloerection – excitement only
	Shoulder bump
	Side roll
	Side turn
	Snarl
	Stand over – during play
	Staring – when interested or curious
	Twist movement
	Yawn - friendly
Yellow	Lip Licking
	Look away
	Muzzle grasp
	Pawing – anticipation or attention-seeking
	Piloerection–neck & shoulders, confident dog
	Scratching
	Shake-off
	Stand over – not accepted by more confident dog
	Standing still
	Staring - alerting
	Yawn – feels uncomfortable or stress
Red	Freezing
	Guarding
	Pawing – on back of more confident dog, not accepted
	Piloerection – full back & tail
	Staring – guarding, targeting, predation, threatening

Guarding

Face Licking

Lip Licking

Look Away

Muzzle Grasp

Pawing

Paw Lift

Snarl

Stand Over

Staring

Twist Movement

Yawn

Back Roll

Piloerection

Side Roll

Side Turn

Chapter 3 –
Play Behaviors

Play is an important dog social activity. Through play, puppies learn about themselves, their limits, and their environment. They learn how to use dog language to avoid conflicts. Play is also an important energy outlet.

Dogs learn dog language and understand how to live peacefully with other dogs by interacting with other dogs. During play, dogs can test behaviors and postures with safe zones to retreat (or hide in) between games (e.g., open crates, pens, play equipment, bushes). Social playgroups provide multiple potential playmates with different experiences and communication skills. For dogs less skilled in body language, well-managed playgroups may help them learn better skills and build their self-confidence.

Understanding the behavior of dogs is vital to running a successful playgroup. Mistakes can result in injuries to both people and dogs. You must learn to intervene before problems occur.

Early intervention is possible only if you understand canine group dynamics and can predict behavior of dogs when they are playing. Chapter 1 and appendix A contain additional information on understanding canine behavior. The information in this chapter will better prepare you to understand play behavior in dogs.

SEPARATING DOGS

Dogs playing off-leash must be placed in suitable play-groups based on the sizes, ages, and temperaments of the dogs in the group.

No matter how well large dogs and small dogs play together, you increase the chance of a serious injury when you put the two together. Large, adolescent dogs often do not have the coordination to avoid stepping on a smaller dog, especially if the larger dogs begin to run.

The canine prey drive affects the interactions of some big and little dogs. Dogs with a strong prey drive will instinctively chase and nip at smaller, active dogs. In an off-leash setting, this type of behavior can quickly get out of control and result in an injury or death. (See Predatory Drift box on page 43.)

Occasionally, large, older or calmer dogs can be placed with small, calm dogs, but the large, rowdy, and adolescent dogs need to be in a separate group. Depending on the sizes of these groups, staff members may want to divide them further to make the groups more manageable.

Puppies under 5 months need their own space until they are large enough to play with the bigger dogs. Off-leash play provides wonderful socialization for puppies, but overwhelming a puppy in a group of large dogs can be detrimental to his social development.

PLAY BEHAVIORS AND GESTURES

The motivation of dogs playing changes very quickly. Proper supervision of the dogs will help identify when the behaviors are becoming more serious and when to intervene to prevent fights. Play movements in dogs include some easily identified behaviors and gestures.

Play Bow

This posture is a solicitation to play. In a play bow, a dog's front legs and chest are low while the rear end is in the air. Some dogs leap toward a dog in an exuberant fake attack that ends in a play bow.

Play bow posture

Exaggerated, Repetitive Movements

You will often see dogs leap wildly into the air or repeat the same spinning motion when they are playing. You know this is play because these exaggerated movements use up more energy than the dog would use if he were actually going to fight.

Exaggerated movements

Lateral Movements

Movement during play is lateral versus forward or backward. Side-to-side motions are common when dogs are playing. Playful dogs will often jump sideways or spin.

The dog on left is jumping and turning laterally toward the other dog.

Low, Slow, Wagging Tail

A low-hanging, slow, relaxed tail wag is usually a friendly sign. A relaxed tail carriage—neither tightly wrapped over the dog's body nor tucked underneath—is best. If this is coupled with a slow, steady, rhythmic wag, that is even better.

Low, relaxed tail carriage

Relaxed, Loose, Curved Bodies

In general, a dog with a relaxed, loose body is in a more playful state than a dog whose body posture is stiff and straight. Although the motion will be fluid and often fast-paced, the ideal play behavior will include dogs who remain relaxed and loose while they are playing.

Balanced Play

The best playing occurs when dogs are fair and balanced in their play. Ideally, the dogs will take turns being on top of one another. They will alternate pinning one another on the ground or jumping on top of one another. Fair and balanced playing is generally relaxed and fluid. Dogs engaging in this sort of play will take breaks from time to time. The dogs will calm themselves down by stopping the play on their own and then resume the play after a momentary pause. This is the best sort of play among dogs in an off-leash setting. If dogs do not play this way on their own, you need to intervene more frequently to ensure the play does not become more aggressive in nature.

PLAY STYLES

Like kids, dogs have their own unique ways of playing. Some dogs prefer a rough and tumble activity, others enjoy wrestling, and still others enjoy quiet, calm interactions. Keep similar play styles together. These styles can be categorized into four basic groups with some variations within each group: chasing, neck biting, cat-like and body-slamming. Some play styles work well together and others do not.

Chasing

This play style involves dogs who like to chase other dogs as well as dogs who enjoy being chased. The game sometimes begins with one dog playfully stalking another. Ideally, you will have at least one dog who chases and one dog who likes to be chased so they can interact together. If you end up with two dogs who both want to chase, but neither wants to be chased, the chasing game never gets underway. Chasing behavior in an off-leash setting can sometimes cause over-excitement in the dogs. Therefore, limit the game to only one or two minutes at a time.

Two dogs playing a chasing game

In addition, watch for dogs who shift into predatory behavior during the chase. A dog who is having fun chasing is relaxed and loose. The dog who becomes predatory looks stiff, fixated, and intense. This type of behavior can easily get out of hand and become aggressive if it is allowed to continue.

Remember the chasing or stalking games require a dog willing to be chased. If one dog is chasing another and the dog being chased is showing signs of stress as discussed in chapter 4, then that dog is not having fun. Such chasing borders on bullying, obnoxious behavior and needs to be redirected.

Neck Biting

Neck-biting is a form of wrestling among dogs. They gently mouth each other's neck, face and ears without force as they play. The neck-biting play style is often seen when the dogs are too tired to get off the floor. Instead, the dogs lie on their sides, head to head, and mouth each other's neck and face. In this type of play, the dogs are loose and relaxed. If a fight were actually going to occur, the dogs would need to stand up first.

PREDATORY DRIFT

Staff members supervising off-leash playgroups need to understand the concept of *predatory drift* when working with dogs. This occurs when a dog's predatory instincts completely rule behavior due to something in the environment. In other words, what starts out as play *drifts into* something predatory.

Predatory drift can occur during chasing games, when the quick motion of a fleeing dog can trigger the chasing dog to attack more aggressively. Predatory drift can also occur when a dog begins making a high-pitched yelping sound. This sound can sometimes trigger other dogs to drift into prey mode to attack the noise-making animal. Predatory drift can be deadly with dogs in an off-leash setting and is more likely to occur in a group containing both large and small dogs together.

This is a fairly benign play style. Interestingly, this is the play style many dog owners find most alarming. When the dogs are grabbing each other's necks, they often show their teeth and make contact with one another's hair and skin. Many dog owners become concerned that this type of play will injure one or both dogs. Educate the clients and your staff on the style of play and point out the relaxed body postures and calm behavior of the dogs in play.

Neck biting while pinning a dog

PINNING A DOG

If one dog pins another to the ground and then freezes on top of him, intervene immediately. This behavior will often cause the bottom dog to panic, and a fight may ensue as the lower dog attempts to get up. While dogs are playing, they may pin one another, but they should relinquish control fairly quickly and begin playing again.

In an ideal situation, there is a balance to the play and the dogs will switch positions, taking turns pinning each other down rather than one dog always pinning the same dog.

Cat-Like

The cat-like play of some of the smaller dogs includes gently batting one another with front paws. Cat-like play can also include quick, exaggerated motions in which dogs spin around one another without touching each other.

Body-Slamming

The body-slamming play style is the primary wrestling play of the larger breed-types. It generally involves dogs knocking into one another, coupled with wrestling on the floor. This play style can be quite rough as dogs slam into one another (as well as the walls of your facility). The body-slamming play style needs to be monitored so the dogs do not become overly stimulated.

The body-slammers usually do not play well with a group of dogs who prefer the cat-like play style. The body-slamming types will have great fun smashing into the smaller breeds. However, little Fifi, the poodle, will not appreciate the antics of Ruckus, the labrador, if they are put in the same playgroup. Despite their high threshold of pain, the body-slamming dogs can hurt themselves if they are allowed to get too rough with one another. Intervene and slow them down from time to time to prevent their play from becoming uncontrollable.

Body slamming can be quite physical.

BREED PLAY STYLES

The American Kennel Club (AKC) categorizes purebred dogs into seven groups. Most dogs are grouped according to their original role or purpose. Play styles in off-leash playgroups are influenced by the dog's breed or job it was originally designed to do. The list below provides some generalizations to help you understand the play styles of dogs of a predominant breed-type.

Sporting Breeds were originally bred to assist in hunting by locating, moving, or bringing back game. The pointing and setting breeds locate game, the spaniels flush or move game, and the retrievers bring game back to the hunters. A few breeds are versatile hunters that combine the talents to locate, flush, and retrieve. Sporting breeds need exercise, enjoy games, and are devoted companions. They generally have a high tolerance to pain and enjoy physical, rowdy play styles.

Hounds were bred to hunt mammals and lead the way in pursuit and catching prey. There are two primary types of hounds: sighthounds pursue by visual cues and scenthounds pursue by sense of smell. There are a few breeds that combine both sight and scent in the hunt. Hounds are generally very comfortable in the pack-like environment of off-leash playgroups.

Working Group dogs were developed to provide protection of homes and livestock and to perform duties requiring strength, intelligence and stamina. Working dogs can be classified as to the tasks of guarding/protecting, sledding, carting, rescue, etc. They are happiest when trained for some type of useful activity. There is a great variation among breeds of this group in temperament, activity level, and suitability for off-leash play.

Terriers were bred to hunt rodents and other pests. Many dogs in the group dig after burrowing animals and have a strong prey drive. Terriers have a reputation as stubborn and brave to a fault. Some have little respect for other dogs and will challenge bigger animals without hesitation. These traits can make terriers a challenge to manage in off-leash playgroups.

Toy Group dogs were specifically bred for human companionship. Many are miniaturized versions of dogs from other groups so it is difficult to assign behavior characteristics to the entire group. Toy dogs thrive on attention and affection. Most have fun-loving temperaments that make them well-suited for playgroups with appropriate sized playmates.

The **Non-Sporting Group** is very diverse and has developed for the breeds that don't fit into the other groups or no longer have a well-used function. Like the toy group, each breed must be evaluated individually as to temperament.

Herding Group dogs have the desire and ability to control the movements of livestock (primarily sheep and cattle). They work with owner's commands and their own judgment to protect and move livestock. Herding is done by stalking, staring, barking, nipping, or gathering the livestock. These breeds are dependable companions and natural watchdogs.

These breeds generally have a high energy level and can sometimes be intimidating to other dogs. They generally like to run and chase.

The following chart classifies some of the most popular AKC breeds by group and management traffic signal for off-leash playgroups. The placement of a particular breed assumes that the individual dog was well socialized as a puppy and has good leadership at home. These are generalizations to help in the early stages of running your playgroups. A dog's breed-type can provide clues on expected temperament and drive, but appropriateness for group play must be assessed for each individual dog.

Group/Breed	Playstyle	Management Tips
	●●(Green)	
Sporting Brittany Springer Spaniel Gr Shorthaired Pt Golden Ret Labrador Ret Weimaraner	Chasing Body-Slamming Neck Biting	Monitor to ensure balanced play; Watch for high arousal and slow down play. High-energy breeds may require mandatory rest breaks.
Sporting Cocker Spaniel	Chasing	Monitor to ensure balanced play
Herding Aus Shepherd Collie Corgi Sheltie	Chasing	Watch for stalking. Excessive barking is a frequent issue; use leadership and management.
Hound Basset Beagle Dachshund	Chasing Neck Biting	Monitor to ensure balanced play
Non-Sporting Bichon Frise Boston Terrier Lhasa Apso Poodle (min) Schipperke	Cat-like Chasing Neck Biting	Monitor to ensure balanced play
Non-Sporting Dalmatian Poodle (std)	Chasing Body-Slamming	Monitor to ensure balanced play; Watch for high arousal and slow down play.
Toy Cav King Charles Maltese Pekingese Pomeranian Poodle Pug Shih Tzu Yorkie*	Cat-like Chasing Neck Biting	Monitor to ensure balanced play *Yorkie breed standard is 7 lb. maximum. High risk of injury so should be matched with similar sized playmates only.
Working Newfoundland Saint Bernard	Chasing Body-Slamming	Monitor to ensure balanced play
Terrier Min Schnauzer Westie	Chasing Neck Biting	Monitor to ensure balanced play

Group/Breed	Playstyle	Management Tips

Herding
  Border Collie
  Ger Shepherd
	Chasing
	Body-
	Slamming
	Neck Biting
		Assert leadership role.
		Staring can scare other dogs
		Watch for stalking.
		Watch for excessive barking

Hound
  Greyhound
  Whippet
	Chasing	Avoid mixing with small fluffy dogs due to prey drive.
		Monitor for over arousal.
		Very thin skin - don't recommend mixing with body-slammers.

Non-Sporting
  Fr Bulldog
  Bulldog
	Chasing
	Body-
	Slamming
		Assert leadership role.
		Monitor to ensure balanced play;
		Watch for high arousal and slow down play.
		Cannot tolerate heat; may require mandatory rest periods. (See additional section on bully breeds).

Non-Sporting
  Am Eskimo
  Chow Chow
  Shar-Pei
	Chasing
	Body-
	Slamming
		Assert leadership role.
		Monitor to ensure balanced play;
		Watch for high arousal and slow down play.

Toy
  Chihuahua
  Min Pinscher
	Cat-like
	Chasing
		Assert leadership: high-spirited & temperamental breeds.
		Monitor to ensure balanced play;
		High risk of injury so put with similar sized playmates only.

Toy Italian Greyhound	Chasing	Very thin skin and legs, don't mix with body-slammers. Can't take cold. Monitor to ensure balanced play;.

Working
  Boxer
  Great Dane
  Mastiff
  Samoyed
  Siberian Husky
	Chasing
	Body-
	Slamming
	Neck Biting
		Assert leadership: confident, independent, possessive, and strong-willed temperaments.
		Monitor to ensure balanced play;
		Watch for high arousal and slow down play.
		May become overly confident when chasing and scare other dogs.

Terrier
  Airedale
  Australian
  Cairn
  Scottish
  Wheaten
	Chasing
	Body-
	Slamming
		Assert leadership: confident, independent, and feisty temperaments.
		Monitor to ensure balanced play;
		Watch for high arousal and slow down play.

Group/Breed	Playstyle	Management Tips
	Red ⬤⬤	
Working Akita Doberman Malamute Rottweiler	Chasing Body-Slamming Neck Biting	Individual dogs often the exception to fitting well in off-leash play. Assert leadership & NILIF (see chapter 7); confident with lower tolerance for other dogs.
Terrier Am Staffordshire Bull Terrier Staffordshire Bull Welsh Terrier Wire Fox Terrier	Chasing Body-Slamming	Individual dogs often the exception to fitting well in off-leash play. Assert leadership & NILIF (see chapter 7); confident with high arousal & prey drives. (See additional section on bully breeds).

Acceptance of Bully Breeds

Bully breeds trace their origins back to the bulldog, bull terrier, or mastiff breeds. Their natural breed temperaments can be challenging in dog social environments and require excellent leadership, control, and management techniques. Breeds typically included in this classification are the English bulldog, American bulldog, American pit bull terrier, American staffordshire terrier, bull mastiff, French bulldog, bull terrier, and boxer.

Acceptance and management of "bully breeds" in off-leash playgroups is an often discussed and debated topic in the industry. Each facility must make the decision whether to accept these dogs based on their facility setup and, more important, on the skill levels of personnel managing the playgroups.

ONE POLICY FOR BULLY BREEDS

Urban Tails dog daycare formalized a bully breed acceptance and management policy after a fight between two bully breeds. Rather than ban specific breeds, the policy focused on the individual dog, management at home, and limits in the daycare environment. Key aspects of this policy:

- Owners of bully breeds/mixes must attend temperament test and demonstrate control of their dog using obedience commands prior to the test.
- Urban Tails trainers will also test dogs' responsiveness to them using commands; very good response to commands and recall is a requirement for admittance to daycare.
- Number of bully breeds/mixes in each playgroup is limited to reduce risk of quick escalation and inappropriate dog behavior (1-2 individual dogs per group based on activity level of the group).
- Escalation levels of groups is monitored and kept very low.
- Bullybreeds/mixes are cycled with mandatory rest periods throughout the play period.
- Bully breeds/mixes are not allowed on any furniture or toys.
- NILIF management program utilized for bully breeds/mixes (see chapter 7 for NILIF information).
- Inappropriate behavior and non-responsiveness are reported to management and training department. Concerns proactively discussed with owners.

INAPPROPRIATE PLAY BEHAVIORS

Play behaviors occur in a continuum. Any play that is allowed to continue uninterrupted for too long has the potential to turn into inappropriate behavior. It is critical to supervise the dogs continuously to prevent this from happening. Some common inappropriate behaviors that may occur in an off-leash setting are listed below. Learning to identify these as early as possible will help prevent the behavior from escalating into aggressive behavior. Chapter 8 contains additional information on controlling a group of dogs off leash.

Bullying

Just as with kids, dogs can pick on one another. Often a bullying dog will pick on a calmer, less active, or less confident dog. Usually the victim is the dog least likely to challenge the bully. A dog who is picking on another dog in an intense manner needs to be redirected for the safety of the group. If you try to move the bully into another group, they will just find another dog to bully. These dogs are not good playgroup candidates. Remember that each dog needs to be having fun. If one dog is having fun and the other dog has his tail constantly tucked, the dogs need to be separated. You do not want the bully to practice his bullying behavior at the expense of another dog. Such behavior helps neither animal.

The dog in back is scaring the dog in front.
Note the stiff muzzle and wide eyes.

Excessive Barking

Some vocalizations will occur in play. However, excessive barking, even in a happy dog, can be annoying to people and other dogs. Dogs who bark due to high arousal levels can create undue stress in the room. Putting these dogs in a quiet room or crate for a few minutes can help decrease their arousal level and reduce the barking. Sometimes, redirecting the dog to another playmate may help as well.

The puppy barking may annoy the older dog who is turning away in an attempt to avoid the puppy.

Too Much Arousal

The term "arousal" when used in conjunction with dog behavior is meant to describe a state of high energy. This can be energy that might occur when a dog is very excited about playing, or it can be energy in which a dog is overly stressed. In a state of high arousal, most dogs will display signs such as dilated pupils; high-pitched, repetitive barking; and/or hyper, nervous behavior, such as pacing or jumping excessively.

The more activity in the room, the higher the arousal level will be. Arousal levels and aggression in dogs are very closely linked. One can easily lead to the other. Therefore, the goal during the playgroup is to keep the arousal level low. When watching the dogs play, be wary of any dog who seems to be overly stimulated.

Sometimes it is easy to confuse the state of high arousal with a highly social dog who just wants to play. A highly aroused dog will usually have dilated pupils, excessive panting, half-moon eyes, and will be more frenetic and stiff than a social dog who is not aroused. Allow the dogs to interact, but do not let them play uninterrupted for long periods of time. Regardless of how well the dogs are playing, watch for signs that the dogs are becoming overly stimulated, stressed and/or aroused. Intervene early and often to prevent the arousal levels from becoming too high.

Dogs Playing Too Rough

A dog playing too roughly with another dog is a problem in an off-leash setting. This is often a result of mismatched play styles and can be resolved by putting the rougher dogs in a different group. If two dogs are playing roughly and enjoying the play, then the behavior is not a problem. However, if one dog is rough and the other dog is trying to hide, neither dog is benefiting and you should intervene.

Mounting

Dogs will sometimes mount one another when playing off leash. There are a wide range of reasons for this behavior including arousal, confidence, nervousness, and anxiety. Most dogs will stop this behavior on their own. However, it is a potential area of tension between dogs, especially if the mounting dog is persistent. In this case, move the dog on top and redirect his play.

Stalking

Stalking behavior sometimes starts as a playful behavior, but can become excessive if it is allowed to continue for too long. If the dog being followed tries to hide and is intimidated, the behavior is becoming a form of bullying.

The stalking behavior can sometimes frighten other dogs.

Head and Chin Over Another Dog's Shoulders

Dogs often posture over one another in an attempt to assert control. One sign of this assertiveness is a dog who puts his chin and head over another dog's shoulders and back. Such behavior does not indicate a fight is about to begin, but nevertheless is a clear sign that one dog is beginning to assert himself over another. If the display is quick, there is no need for concern. However, if the display continues and the movements become more forceful, then intervention is necessary.

The dog on right puts his head and chin over the other dog.

Pushing a Dog to the Point of Submission

Anytime a dog continues to push himself on another dog, even after the dog shows signs of avoidance, you need to intervene. If a dog is being chased and then ends up becoming overwhelmed and hiding, the chasing dog needs to be redirected. If two dogs are playing and one nips the other, causing a yelp, both dogs should stop playing on their own. If they do not stop, you need to intervene and help them play nicely or place them in separate playgroups.

PUTTING IT ALL TOGETHER

The various play gestures and behaviors discussed in this chapter can be seen in the chart below using our off-leash play management traffic signal.

Mgmt Signal	Play Gesture
Green	Play bow
	Lateral movements
	Exaggerated, repetitive movements
	Low, slow, wagging tail
	Neck biting play
	Cat-like play
	Balanced play
Yellow	Chase
	Pinning a dog & quickly releases
	Body-slamming play
	Excessive barking
	Increase in arousal
	Rough play
	Mounting
	Stalking
	Head & chin over shoulders
Red	Pinning a dog with no release
	High arousal
	Bullying
	Play that is hurting or scaring a dog
	Stalking that scares a dog
	Pushing a dog to submission

Chapter 4 –
Stress in Dogs

Just like humans, dogs can become stressed in a wide variety of situations. They may show stress with the unfamiliar, when threatened or when in pain. They may get stressed when we are angry or punish them. Excitement can also cause stress such as meeting a new dog at playgroup. An active and aroused group of dogs playing can stress a dog. But keep in mind, dogs get stressed for the same reason we do–when they feel unable to cope.

It is important to be able to identify the signs of stress because an increase in stress reduces an animal's tolerance level. In other words, a dog who is stressed is more likely to show extreme fear and/or aggressive behavior than a dog who is not. Learning to identify signs of stress will help you monitor the dogs in your care and help you make decisions about how to best manage them.

Scientific research has given us some information about stress. When a stressful incident occurs, the body's defense mechanism reacts to help the animal take action. The production of adrenaline and other hormones increases the body's breathing, heart rate, and blood pressure to allow oxygen-rich blood to quickly move to the brain and muscles. This gives the body energy to respond.

During a stressful situation, an animal becomes more aware of his surroundings and is less sensitive to pain. At the same time, unneeded bodily functions shut down. Reproduction and growth systems, including the immune system, shut down to allow the body more energy to concentrate on coping with the stress.

All these physiological responses occur in dogs when they are under stress. Their bodies prepare for defense, they become more aware of their surroundings, and they are less sensitive to pain. In this heightened state of arousal, dogs are more likely to react suddenly in ways that might not be safe in a group setting. Dogs under stress are more likely to show inappropriate playgroup behaviors, such as lunging, growling, fighting, or biting.

Since we can't rely on scientific testing of adrenaline counts and hormone measurements to tell us the level of stress in an off-leash group setting, we must rely on the physical changes in a dog's body to identify when the dog is under stress. Being able to recognize stress in dogs will greatly increase your ability to run a successful off-leash play session.

IS IT STRESS OR IS IT NORMAL?

Many dogs will show various, brief stress signals throughout their playtime activities. Use these signals as guides and act on them accordingly to prevent problems in the playgroup. However, a dog who is showing one sign is not necessarily overwhelmed. The key is to observe and understand how many stress signals a dog is showing. If there are many signals, try to reduce the source of stress for the dog. Also, as you get to know the dogs in your care, you will be able to identify what is normal behavior and what is more extreme for each particular dog.

STRESS SIGNALS

Stress signals indicate that a dog is uncomfortable. There are several theories on why dogs use stress signals. Some say they are used to help the dog calm down, others say they are used to calm down animals in the environment. Regardless of the reason, we can use stress signals as an early identification system to help us ensure dogs are playing safely.

SOCIALIZATION

Although all dogs will experience moments of mild stress in new situations, a dog who is overwhelmed and remains stressed in an off-leash play situation should be dismissed from the group. Excessively shy or nervous dogs may not benefit from a large playgroup. These dogs need controlled training environments with very specific playmates to help them boost their confidence. Most off-leash play sessions are not organized in a manner that allows for controlled behavior modification of this type. Be aware when your playgroup may be doing more harm than good for a shy or nervous dog, especially a puppy. See appendix B for more information on the development stages of dogs.

Be careful not to let dogs become too overwhelmed.

Stress-free dogs playing happily show relaxed, curved body language. They display playful, loose body postures, and their breathing patterns are normal. Conversely, nervous or stressed dogs have rigid, tight bodies. They generally close their mouths, stiffen their bodies, and often have a change in breathing pattern.

This chapter contains an alphabetized list of some easily recognizable signals dogs may show as they move from a relaxed state to a more nervous or anxious state. Be aware that dog behavior is very fluid. It happens quickly, and you need to learn to identify signals as they occur. You will often see combinations of signals. In fact, combinations of stress signals are more worrisome than one specific signal.

Clawing/Jumping
Some dogs will claw and jump at people and/or other dogs when they are nervous. At first glance, this appears to be inappropriate behavior from an untrained dog. However, in a stressed dog, this behavior takes on a more panic-stricken feel. These dogs are looking for help and need relief from whatever is causing them stress.

Closed Mouth
Generally speaking, a relaxed dog's first sign of nervousness is to close his mouth in a slightly tense pose. When a dog is panting, the closed mouth is easily seen because the panting will stop suddenly as he waits to determine if further action is warranted. Be careful when a dog pants, closes his mouth, and then does not relax again. This indicates the dog is nervous or stressed. A closed mouth is a very easy signal to observe, but the average pet owner rarely recognizes it as a sign of stress.

Open Mouth   *Closed Mouth*

These two dogs are looking at the same thing, but one is more worried than the other.

Dilated Pupils

It can sometimes be hard to see dilated pupils from a distance. However, you can usually see light reflecting in a dog's eyes when the pupils are dilated. Look for excessive reflection in the dog's eyes to recognize the stressed dog with dilated pupils.

Note the reflection and dilated pupils.
This dog also has half-moon eye,
closed mouth, and ears back.

Drooling

Excessive drooling (in the absence of food) can often be a sign of stress. Some dogs may show no other outward signs of stress other than long strings of drool that drop from the mouth.

Half-Moon Eye

In most dogs, you rarely see the whites around the outside of the eyes. When the eyes begin to get larger and the dog's face becomes tense, the whites of the eyes are more apparent. The whites also become more pronounced if the dog holds his head still, but looks out of the corner of his eye at something that makes him nervous.

Note the half-moon eye, curled lips, flattened ears, and tight muzzle.

Lip Licking

This signal is very easy to see, but is rarely recognized as a sign of stress by dog owners. The dog will flick his tongue out and lick his lips or nose. Pay attention not only to the fact that the dog is licking his lips, but how quickly it happens. Generally speaking, the more stress the dog is experiencing, the faster the lip licking. Dogs licking their lips often have tight muzzles, another sign of tension.

Lip licking

Look Away

A dog who turns his head to avoid direct eye contact may be stressed. When dogs get scared, they will often turn away from what is scaring them. A dog avoiding eye contact may be saying, "Hey, I don't want to interact with you." Forcing the dog to interact when he is trying to avoid eye contact may result in growling or snapping. The dog is asking for some space. Respect his request and give him time and space to relax. Some dogs will rebound right away; other dogs need more time. Often, when a dog looks away, he will also lower his head slightly.

Look away, half-moon eye, and closed mouth

Panting/Change in Breathing Pattern

Dogs playing will obviously become tired and begin to pant more. This is to be expected. However, watch for dogs whose panting appears excessive or tense. Dogs who enter the playgroup and begin panting even before they have started to play may be stressed. Dogs who become too excited or aroused may begin panting more heavily in shorter breaths. This may be a sign of stress. Tightly held tongues, tense muzzles, and prominent muscles and veins on the face indicate more stress and not just exhaustion panting.

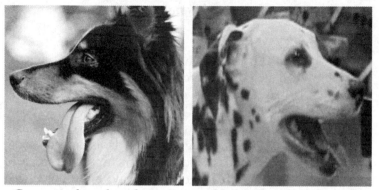

Compare the relaxed, panting in the dog on left to the tense panting in the stressed dog on the right. Note tension in tongue, muzzle and backward ears in dog on right.

Piloerection (Raised Hackles)

This term refers to a dog's hair standing up on end. Many people assume this behavior means a dog is aggressive, but that is not always the case. Dogs who display piloerection are usually becoming over-stimulated through play, or they may be nervous or scared. Either way, it is best to intervene to give them time to settle down.

This dog's hackles are up as a stranger approaches.

Scratching/Sniffing/Stretching

Does the dog show interest in something and then suddenly begin scratching, sniffing, or stretching? These are all ways in which dogs relieve their stress or deflect attention and frustration. Obviously dogs scratch, sniff, and stretch for other reasons as well. However, when any of these behaviors occur out of context to the situation, they are probably related to stress. For example, a client tells their dog to sit and the dog suddenly feels the urge to scratch his neck.

Shaking Off

It is normal for a dog to shake off after a bath. However, when a dog shakes off and he's not wet, it's usually a way of releasing stress. It's a dog's way of saying, "Wow, kind of stressful...I need to hit the reset button." This is similar to person who might be placed in a stressful environment and then say, "Whew, I need to shake it off." In a playgroup, take note when a dog meets a person or another dog, sniffs, and then moves away and shakes off.

Yawning

Dogs yawn in many situations and in a wide variety of ways. Sometimes they will do little half yawns in an attempt to relax. Owners typically think yawning usually means the dog is tired or bored. However, yawning usually indicates some level of stress. In a playgroup, yawning normally means a dog is not interested in playing.

Yawning

WHAT CAN MAKE A DOG STRESSED?

- Direct threats (by us or other dogs)
- Violence, anger, aggression in their environment
- Jerking on the leash, pushing them down, pulling them along
- Too many demands in training and daily life
- Overstimulation (too much rowdy play)
- No energy outlet, a dog cooped up all day long
- New or unfamiliar environments
- Hunger, thirst
- Pain and illness
- Too much noise
- Being alone
- Sudden scary situations
- Never being able to relax, always being disturbed

HANDLING STRESS IN A PLAYGROUP

When a dog is reacting to stress in his environment, your goal is to reduce the dog's stress level. In order to stop the stress signal from occurring, you need to remove the stress in the environment. Find the reasons for the dog to be stressed by looking critically at yourself, the other dogs in the area, and your surroundings. Then modify the environment to help the dog.

The dog may need a break from the play or perhaps just a new playmate. Sometimes dogs will show signs of stress when they first arrive in the playgroup and need time to settle into their new activity.

In general, if you begin to see a dog with many stress signals, it is time to intervene. Any dog that is under stress is more likely to show aggression. You must be able to identify these signals quickly and use them as early signs for intervention. See chapter 8 for additional information about controlling a group of dogs interacting off leash.

OTHER WAYS TO IDENTIFY A DOG LIVING IN STRESS

Dogs show stress through some of the signals we've discussed. Behaviorally, a dog living in a high state of stress will show some larger patterns of behavior.

- Inability to calm down, restless
- Overreaction to things happening (e.g., doorbell ringing or a dog approaching)
- Scratching
- Biting themselves
- Barking, howling, whining
- Diarrhea
- Smell – both mouth or body giving off a bad odor
- Sudden "attack" of dandruff
- Shaking
- Obsessive-compulsive behaviors
- Excessive shedding
- Housetraining accidents

WHAT CAN WE DO ABOUT DOGS LIVING IN STRESS?

- Change environment and routines wherever possible
- Stop using harsh methods in training and handling
- Learn to identify, and reduce stress signals
- Avoid putting the dog in a situation of hunger, thirst, heat, or extreme cold
- Provide ample opportunities for them to relieve themselves in appropriate areas
- Find balance of exercise and activity
- Let the dog be part of his pack as much as possible; allow your dog to be with you or someone in the family, and teach them gradually to accept being alone
- Closeness, touching, massage, essentially being together without being held by force

Chapter 5 –
Aggression

Aggression can show up in a variety of ways. The term is used far too often to mean dogs actually fighting. In reality, there are wide ranges of behaviors that constitute aggressive displays. These displays do not mean a dog should be labeled an aggressive dog. They only mean that, in a certain instance, in relation to another dog, human, or situation, the dog is motivated to show an aggressive behavior.

In fact, some aggressive displays are completely appropriate for the situation. For instance, a mother dog who growls at her puppy for jumping on her head is showing appropriate aggression. If she bit and injured the puppy, she would not be showing appropriate aggression.

You need to learn how to distinguish between what is normal and appropriate and what is not. You also need to recognize those threat displays that require staff intervention to prevent an escalation in the aggressive behavior.

FIGHTING
Normal playing includes a great deal of play-biting and wrestling between the dogs. However, these games can sometimes escalate into more serious scraps if you and your staff do not monitor the dogs closely. By getting to know the dogs and learning how they play, you will be able to identify which dogs to watch more closely than others.

FACTORS THAT INFLUENCE AGGRESSIVE BEHAVIOR

Several factors can affect the relative level of aggression a dog will display in any threatening situation.

- **Learned Behavior**–if showing aggression has resulted in the scary person or dog going away, the behavior has been reinforced and is likely to occur again.
- **Genetics**–Certain breeds are hard-wired for aggressive behavior. They are often more likely to show strong aggressive behaviors.
- **Hormones**–Testosterone can cause a stronger aggressive reaction in dogs. Females in season or with litters may be more prone to aggression.
- **Social Development Periods**–Well-socialized, even-tempered dogs are less likely to show aggressive behaviors than dogs who were isolated during critical social periods.
- **Stress and Fear**–Like people, dogs are more likely to show aggression when they are under stress or when they are scared.

Fights in playgroups don't happen out of the blue. There are early warning signals that occur when a fight is imminent. In general, if you think the playing seems serious, stop the game before it escalates. Do not wait until the dogs are in a full-blown fight before you attempt to intervene. Distracting the dogs will quickly end most tiffs or scuffles. However, waiting until a fight occurs will require much more work to stop.

It is important to keep written records of any aggressive displays in a playgroup. This documentation will help determine the course of action to take with a particular dog or group of dogs. In order to standardize some of the language used for dog incidents, some common terms are defined below.

INJURIES IN A PLAYGROUP

In an off-leash play situation, injuries may occur that have nothing to do with a dog-aggression incident. Sometimes accidents occur during play. All injuries should be documented. Supervision will help to determine whether a dog incident occurred. Here are some key points to consider when documenting an injury:

- A nick on the ear is often an accident
- A surface nick on the face, neck, or thigh may be a result of normal dog play
- A deep puncture wound anywhere is cause for concern (poor bite inhibition)
- More than one puncture during a fight or more than one fight is a major concern

---

Snark

A snark is characterized by a big aggressive display that usually includes strong vocalizations from one dog to another where the receiving dog does not vocalize or fight back. In this situation, the snarky dog may be saying "My ball!," "You're scaring me," or "I told you to stop it!" Often snarking is appropriate. However, if it is continuous or if it occurs to a dog who is not tolerant, it can cause an escalation in aggression between the dogs.

Tiff

A tiff is an aggressive-sounding moment between two dogs in which both dogs vocalize. In this situation, both dogs are arguing with each other. One dog may have violated another's space or stepped on another dog. Again, most tiffs are appropriate, but if they seem to occur consistently between two dogs they could escalate.

Scuffle

A scuffle is a very brief aggressive interaction between two or more dogs that includes body movements and not just vocalizations. Scuffles are not long or intense. You can usually stop a scuffle by making a loud noise or it ends on its own within seconds. Most scuffles do not result in injuries. They are often escalations of tiffs that have occurred too often.

Fight

A fight occurs when two dogs hash it out over status or control of some resource. Fights last more than 10 seconds and often require intervention to end. A fight may or may not result in injuries. However, they are not desirable in an off-leash play environment.

LETTING THE DOGS WORK IT OUT

Letting dogs work out their squabbles in an off-leash setting isn't wise. Allowing the dogs to work it out may result in a fight involving the whole group of dogs, not just the ones that are trying to work things out. In addition, an incorrect assumption that the dogs will work things out without actually fighting may result in an injury to a dog who does not belong to you. You are there to keep the dogs safe and to intervene rather than letting dogs work out their own issues.

AGGRESSIVE DISPLAYS THAT PRECEDE A FIGHT

Stress signals are your first clue that a dog is getting nervous or anxious. In addition, inappropriate play behaviors are early clues that trouble is brewing. See chapters 3 and 4 for more information about play and stress. Warning signals, often occurring in conjunction with stress signals, are generally immediate precursors to a fight. You need to be able to differentiate between stress and warning signals. Warning signals are a little more serious and require immediate intervention. Some of the more obvious warning signals are included below.

Stiffness

A dog who is stiff is usually tense and stressed. The rigidity may be seen in a stiff-legged stance or tightly flexed hindquarters. You can also see tension in the face and muzzle. Usually this tension will appear in the form of veins or muscles tightening on the face or a furrowed brow.

Both these dogs are under stress.
The dog on the left displays stress in a yawn.
The dog on the right is stiffening in a more offensive pose.

Freezing

In general, when a dog's body becomes tense or rigid, it indicates nervousness or stress. Initial signs of tension will happen very quickly. A dog may appear to hold his breath for a second and then relax again. Heed this warning and intervene if necessary. If a dog becomes more nervous, the tension in his body will begin to increase, and he will hold his position for longer. Be careful of any dog who is extremely tense when interacting with other people or dogs. Dogs usually freeze when they enter a state of nervousness that begins to border on fight or flight.

Direct Stare

Watch for a dog who seems intently focused on another dog or engages in excessive, aggressive stalking. If the dog's stare is frozen and stiff, especially if the rest of the body is stiff, intervene to distract the dog. Staring without blinking is often a precursor to an aggressive display.

The dog on the right has staring eyes, closed muzzle, erect ears, and a furrowed brow.

Snarling

Far too often, humans ignore the tiny muzzle movements associated with a lip snarl. Ideally, dogs will use as little force as possible to end an unpleasant encounter. This means, dogs will often lift their lip in a snarl before they growl or snap. If this happens, it is important that you identify the behavior and intervene immediately. Do not make the dog increase his aggressive posture because you did not heed the snarl. Lip-curling movements in the dog's muzzles can be very small. Observe all of them and intervene regardless of the size of snarl. It is a clear signal that the dog is uncomfortable.

A snarl can be a small muzzle motion or a much larger one.

POSTURING: IS IT NORMAL OR NOT?

As you begin to observe dogs more closely, you will find wide variations in these warning signals. How do you know if the signal is normal posturing behavior that will end, or if it is a precursor to a fight that should be redirected?

Generally speaking, if the behavior changes quickly and the dogs become relaxed and playful again, then the behavior is normal playing. Continue to monitor the play. However, if the behavior intensifies, intervene.

A good clue to the intensity of the dog's behavior is to watch both the dog giving the signal and the dog receiving the signal. If a dog is displaying some warning signal and the other dog backs away, the behavior will probably end on its own. On the other hand, if the receiver becomes more challenging, the interaction could escalate.

With experience you will begin to see subtle, but dramatic differences in the dogs, and you will know when intervention is most important.

Growling

Dogs will sometimes growl in play. These playful growls are accompanied by loose, relaxed body postures, low tail carriage, and desirable play behaviors and movements. When growling is accompanied by a direct stare, freezing, or stiffening, or if it is deep and low, the behavior needs to be addressed immediately. Redirect the growling dog(s) and reduce the tension. There are times when one dog will growl, and another dog will begin to bark at him. This can cause the growling dog to retaliate with aggression directed at the barking dog, even if the original growl was directed at a different dog. Growling tells you the dog is reaching the end of his rope. He needs your help.

RESOURCE GUARDING

Dogs sometimes guard the things they find valuable. Experts call this practice *resource guarding*. You need to understand and identify resource guarding behaviors because fights between dogs for control of resources can become very violent.

The important thing to understand about resource guarding is that the value of an item is very subjective. Not all dogs will guard the same items. Resources can include obvious items such as food or treats, but can also extend to other valuable commodities: water, toys, favorite sleeping spots, and people. Dogs can even guard things people consider disgusting, such as dog feces and vomit.

This dog guards his toy.

Because we cannot always identify exactly what a particular dog will consider valuable, you need to be able to identify the signs of resource guarding.

Many of the stress signals mentioned in chapter 4 and the warning signals mentioned in this chapter apply to resource guarding behaviors. The signs are coupled with obvious attachments to a space, person, toy, or food. If the item is in the dog's possession, he will normally hover over it, circle it, or stand near or on it. If you notice dogs leaning against or circling you, sometimes growling at other dogs who come close, the dog is guarding you. If a dog is lying on a bed and growls when other dogs approach, the dog is guarding his bed. Watch for early signs such as freezing, lip licking, and curling the lip because those signs almost always precede the more obvious signals of growling, lunging, and barking.

In most cases, removing the resource will resolve the problem. If the dog is guarding a person, the person needs to walk away from the dog; if the dog is guarding a bed, the bed can be removed from the room.

STOPPING A DOG FIGHT

Your primary job is to identify early-warning signs of aggression and intervene before a fight occurs. If you have properly screened dogs and are diligent in monitoring play, fights will be infrequent. However, do plan in advance how you will react if a fight occurs. Regardless of the method used, the potential for a person to get bitten is great. Proceed with caution in any fighting situation.

DO NOT PUNISH THE GROWL

Human beings are hard-wired to discipline undesirable behavior. It is in our nature. If you understand that signals leading toward aggression are on a continuum from subtle signs, such as freezing, lip licking, and growling, to more obvious signs, such as lunging and biting, you will understand why it is important not to punish dogs when they show aggression.

Ideally, we want dogs to use as little force as possible when they decide to display signs of aggression. If a dog curls his lip at me or growls and I back away, I have taught the dog that low levels of aggression work. Do I want to teach a dog that aggression works? Not necessarily…but in that instant, when I am getting the lip curl or the growl, I have reached a critical point in which I am no longer in a training mode. I will move away to avoid a situation in which the dog's aggression must escalate. I now know I must start training to prevent this behavior from reoccurring and can use my experience to define future training protocols.

However, if I punish that lip curl or the growl, I have done nothing except teach the dog that low levels of aggression do not work. This may cause the dog to escalate to higher levels of aggression immediately in the next similar situation. This is how you can end up with dogs who seem to bite without warning. That is definitely not what I want in a playgroup because I rely on my staff's skills of observation to keep the dogs safe.

Reading the dogs is the key to the staff's success, so do not punish the dogs for providing you with information you need. If a dog is growling in an off-leash setting, you should reconsider his attendance. Also recommend the client contact a trainer through the Association of Pet Dog Trainers (www.apdt.com) for help.

If the dogs get into a fight, attempt to break them up by using water first. Try spraying the dogs with water from a squirt bottle, dumping water from a bowl onto the fighting dogs, or spray them with a hose, if available. If that does not work, make a loud noise (most effective by dropping a metal bowl on the ground or using an air horn). You can also try using Direct Stop, a citronella based animal deterrent sold by Premier® Pet Products. Sometimes throwing blankets or coats over the fighting dogs can startle them enough to make them stop fighting momentarily.

REDIRECTED AGGRESSION

Be careful in any instance in which a dog is showing aggression. Though the aggression may be directed at another animal, dogs can become frustrated and redirect their aggression onto any animal or person who is nearby. The new victim could be you, a staff member, or another dog.

If none of those measures stops the fight, you may need to physically intervene. This is quite risky because many dogs will bite you during a fight. If possible, grab the back legs and quickly pull the dogs apart and let go of them immediately. As soon as the dogs are separated, *crate each dog involved*, no matter which dog started the fight. Check each animal for injuries and treat as necessary. Also check yourself and the staff members who helped break up the fight to see if anyone was injured. Leave the dogs crated for a minimum of 15 to 20 minutes. When they are released from the crate, supervise them to ensure they do not begin fighting again. Depending on the seriousness of the incident, consider the dogs' removal from the playgroup for the day or permanently.

GROUP MENTALITY
One problem with a fight between dogs in an off-leash playgroup is the group mentality that occurs when a fight

occurs. In addition to crating the fighting dogs, tether or crate all dogs in the room. Be wary of the smaller, shyer dogs. In the heat of the action, they will often find the courage to begin fighting as well. The group mentality that erupts when a fight breaks out is very dangerous and is one of the main reasons for proactive supervision and early intervention. Always have an employee in the room with any loose dogs. The ideal ratio is 1 person for every 10 to 15 dogs depending on the size of the dogs and the experience of the staff.

One of the biggest decisions after a fight is whether to expel the fighting dogs from the playgroup. Many factors should be taken into consideration in making this decision. If the dogs have been involved in numerous minor incidents in the past, then perhaps they would be best in a pet sitting or daytime boarding situation instead of an off-leash playgroup. If the dogs just seem to dislike one another, then arranging for them to attend at different times may manage the situation and prevent further altercations. The dog's bite inhibition is also an important consideration in the decision on whether or not to expel the dog.

BITE INHIBITION

Dogs use their mouths all day long during play. They have an amazing ability to control the level of their bite if they have learned to do so. On the other hand, a dog who intends to inflict injury can do so with amazing speed. Any altercation in which a dog causes a serious puncture to another dog needs to be reviewed. These injuries are usually considered grounds for the permanent removal of a dog from a playgroup. A dog who leaves a deep puncture on another dog has little bite inhibition and is not safe to have in an off-leash environment. The chart on the next page is a guide to evaluating a dog's bite inhibition.

DR. IAN DUNBAR'S BITE LEVEL ASSESSMENT *(printed with permission)*	
#1	Obnoxious or aggressive behavior, but no skin-contact by teeth.
#2	Skin-contact by teeth, but no skin-puncture. However there may be nicks (less than 1/10" deep) and slight bleeding caused by forward or lateral movement of teeth against skin, but no vertical punctures.
#3	One to four punctures from a single bite with no puncture deeper than half the length of the dog's canine teeth. May be lacerations in a single direction, caused by victim pulling away, owner pulling dog away, or gravity (little dog jumps, bites, and drops to floor)
#4	One to four punctures from a single bite with at least one puncture deeper than half the length of the dog's canine teeth. May also have deep bruising around the wound (dog held on for *x* seconds and bore down) or lacerations in both directions (dog held on and shook its head from side to side).
#5	Multiple-bite incident with at least two Level 4 bites.
#6	Flesh consumed or victim dead.
In general, there is a huge transition between appropriate versus inappropriate use of the mouth when you cross into level 3 and above. Dogs who display inappropriate bite inhibition (level 3 and above) need training and should not be in an off-leash setting.	

WHAT TO ASK YOURSELF AFTER A FIGHT

Anytime there is a serious fight, you must review what happened in order to ensure the situation will not happen again. Were there problems with staff supervision? Was the staff negligent in its duties? Were there early-warning signs that went unnoticed? Was there intervention that should have been used to prevent the fight? Safety is everyone's responsibility and the input of your staff in regard to these questions can help to improve your policies and enhance your facility.

How to prevent aggression in the playgroup environment:

- Supervise the dogs. Don't leave dogs unattended where they can practice inappropriate behaviors.
- Provide structure for the dogs. Encourage them to take breaks and don't allow dogs to play uninterrupted for long periods of time.
- Teach your staff to understand dog body language.

Chapter 6 – Greetings

One of the most important steps in any playgroup will be the initial introduction of new dogs into the group. The introduction process is a critical step to ensuring only well-mannered, appropriate dogs are placed together to play. Introductions are often the most stressful time for new staff members.

PRESCREENING DOGS

There are some helpful pre-screening questions you can use to assess dogs coming into a playgroup for the first time. Dog daycares usually have an evaluation form that owners complete prior to a dog attending daycare. Facilities offering playgroup sessions might not have a formal written report, but some basic questions can be asked verbally to owners when they attend for the first time. This chapter will help you identify red-flag items that might need clarification before allowing a dog to play off leash. Some items will rule out a dog's participation in an off-leash setting even without seeing him play.

How old is your dog?

This gives you information on possible prior experience the dog has had in playgroups. It will also give you some information on the energy level the dog may have. Generally speaking, a puppy under 5 months of age is not usually a concern. However, puppies need to play with other puppies and well-socialized adult dogs who will not scare or bully the younger dogs.

Adolescent dogs (6 months to 2 years old) are going to have more energy than older dogs. Anticipate a rowdier group if you have many adolescent dogs together.

A possible red-flag answer to this question is a dog over 7. Older dogs sometimes do not enjoy the high energy levels of many playgroups. This can be handled by offering a calmer playgroup. Some dog daycares also offer rooms where older dogs can lounge around and play with less intensity.

Why do you think your dog would like daycare/ playgroups?

If the dog is still a puppy, an owner will probably tell you they are bringing their dog to play in order to get socialization. This is a great reason to bring a dog to an off-leash play setting. Puppies can benefit by playing with other well-socialized dogs. However, if the owner is bringing an adult dog for socialization, this is often a red-flag answer. If an adult dog "needs socialization," you can sometimes assume that the dog has had some dog-to-dog issue and the owner is trying to fix the problem. For these dogs, off-leash playgroups may not be the best option unless you are able to provide proper behavior modification within the constraints of your play session. Many owners believe dog-aggression issues will be resolved in an off-leash setting. This is not usually the case. These dogs are typically not suitable for off-leash play.

MY DOG LOVES TO PLAY WITH OTHER DOGS

Some owners will bring their dogs to a playgroup because they claim their dog loves to play with other dogs. While this might be true, it's important for you to confirm that assessment.

Many owners are not aware of subtle dog body language that may indicate a dog is overwhelmed or nervous. Sometimes dogs who seem to enjoy playing (from the owner's point of view) are merely overly aroused or anxious. It is up to the you to educate the owners if necessary.

Has your dog played with other dogs? If so, how many dog "friends" does your dog have?

In assessing the answer to this question, look specifically for whether a dog has played with a wide variety of dogs or only one or two other dogs. A possible red-flag answer to this question is a dog who has played primarily with the dog next door. A dog who has played every day with one other dog will often be described as "a dog who loves to play with other dogs." In reality, this might be a dog who loves to play only with one particular well-known dog and may not enjoy meeting new dogs. On the other hand, if the dog has played with a wide variety of other dogs at dog parks, dog daycares, or while traveling, the dog may have an easier time adjusting to an off-leash playgroup setting.

SHY OR NERVOUS DOGS

There is no doubt that shy and nervous dogs can benefit from playing with well-matched playmates. However, putting these dogs in a group that is overwhelming or crowded can ruin the dog's future social interactions with other dogs. Not all playgroups can be set up to accommodate the shy or nervous dog.

If you cannot provide proper behavior modification for these types of dogs, do not allow them in your playgroup. These dogs normally need more one-on-one play rather than group play when they first start out. See the stress signals in chapter 4 to identify when a dog is overwhelmed and should be removed from the play setting.

How does your dog usually play?

This question can often indicate a dog's play style. If an owner tells you the dog loves to crash into dogs (a body-slamming style), you probably won't put the dog with the calmer, gentler players. Possible red-flag answers to this question include a description that the dog "likes to be in charge," "likes to have things his way," or "wants to be alpha." These terms often describe a more confident dog who may challenge or bully other dogs in the group. For more information on play styles, see chapter 3.

What does your dog do when he gets upset?

Very few owners will describe their dog as aggressive. Owners do not think in terms of aggression unless they've had an aggressive dog before. However, owners often use some common phrases when describing a dog with aggressive tendencies. Common phrases include:

- He gets grumpy
- He's growly
- He doesn't like it
- He'll let you know
- He gets a "look" in his eye
- You can just tell

All of these phrases should be viewed as red flags. Inquire more about what situations cause the dog to act this way. If a dog does these behaviors in response to handling by people or when playing with other dogs, he may not be suitable for an off-leash playgroup.

Using our management traffic signal chart, we can categorize some of the answers to these prescreening questions.

Question	Response	Concerns
	Green	
How old is your dog?	5 months and under	Bad experiences can negatively affect them for life. Place with other puppies and well-socialized adults only.
Why do you think your dog would like playgroups?	Socialization (for a puppy)	Bad experiences can negatively affect them for life. Place with other puppies and well-socialized adults only.
Has your dog played with other dogs? How many?	Yes, has played with a wide variety of dogs	Confirm enjoyment by watching dog play.
How does your dog usually play?	Wrestling, body slamming, chasing, etc. (a type of play style is indicated)	Gives you guidance as to where to place the dog in the playgroups.
	Yellow	
How old is your dog?	6 months – 2 years	Watch arousal levels during play.
Why do you think your dog would like playgroups?	Socialization (for an adult dog)	Often means the dog is having dog-to-dog issues. An off-leash setting may not be appropriate without behavior modification.
Has your dog played with other dogs? How many?	Plays often with the dogs next door	This may be a dog who enjoys the familiar dogs, but doesn't necessarily like meeting new dogs, especially if this is an older dog.

Question	Response	Concerns
	Red	
How old is your dog?	7 years or older	A red flag unless you can offer a room for calmer, older dogs or the dog is very well-socialized with other dogs.
How does your dog usually play?	Likes to be in charge, likes to have things his way	May indicate a bully that is not appropriate in an off -leash setting.
What does your dog do when he gets upset?	Gets grumpy or growly, doesn't like it, he'll let you know, he gets a "look" in his eye, you can just tell	May indicate a dog with potential aggressive tendencies that may not be suitable in an off-leash setting with other dogs and strangers

This prescreening process should take just a moment or two once you are comfortable identifying red-flag answers. Any red flags should be addressed in more detail with the owner. Based on the experience of your staff, you will then decide whether or not to try an actual introduction with a new dog.

The chart below depicts the prescreening process in a flow chart form.

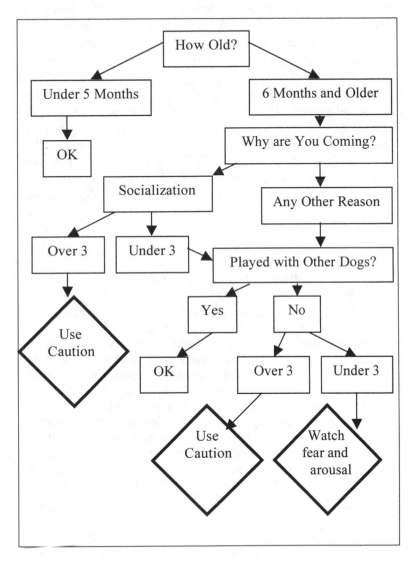

DOING THE INTRODUCTION

During initial introductions, dogs should only meet one dog at a time. When you force a new dog into a larger group of unknown dogs, the arousal and excitement level will be higher than necessary. That sort of setting can easily overwhelm even a well-mannered dog.

As discussed in chapter 1, greeting rituals are very important for social animals as they are programmed to be suspicious of the unfamiliar. This is why dogs, like humans, actively engage in ritualized greeting behaviors. The goal of the greeting is to assure one another of peaceful intentions (in most instances). During an initial greeting, pointing the body, head, or eyes at another dog signals confidence or higher rank and can be a threat. Turning the body, head, or eyes away is a pacifying, appeasement gesture.

HOW TO DO THE INTRODUCTIONS

There are several different methods for introducing a new dog to your playgroup. You might introduce a new dog off-leash, on-leash or perhaps through a fence. Each method has its own advantages and disadvantages. You will need to evaluate your staff's strengths and weaknesses to determine which method is best for your facility. Regardless of the method used, introduce a new dog slowly and carefully one dog at a time. Start by allowing the new dog to get accustomed to a small group of non-reactive dogs. Add more dogs as the new dog becomes more relaxed. A poorly managed introduction can ruin a dog's experience in a playgroup and prevent him from adjusting to an off-leash play environment.

Greeting Ritual

In an ideal greeting, dogs will approach one another sideways rather than head on. Next, they will sniff muzzles, necks, and move down to sniff genital and rear area. A variation in the greeting ritual can be the first sign of a problem between two dogs. If one or both dogs freeze and fail to continue the ritual, redirect them by calling them to you. A halt in the sequence can sometimes indicate fear or aggression is brewing. Try not to pull the dogs away with a leash or collar because this can cause frustration and lead to aggression. Instead, use your voice to encourage them to come to you, even if they are on a leash. After a minute or two, allow the dogs to start over.

Dogs who are equal in age and rank may proceed to play quickly after this greeting ritual. In other cases, the lower ranking dog normally displays subordinate pacifying gestures first. The higher-ranking dog may respond with friendly, appeasement behaviors. In a friendly, polite greeting, you will see body postures that are neutral and balanced. A dog who abruptly sits when approached may be feeling nervous or overwhelmed.

Sideways Approach

Sniffing Necks

Sniffing Necks

Sniffing Rear End

WHAT TO EXPECT WHEN DOGS MEET

New dogs' behavior will range from *scared to death* to *ready to play immediately*. Even dogs who have played in other dog parks or daycares may need time to adjust to new surroundings. It is perfectly normal for new dogs to be slow to initiate play. If they prefer to hide for a period of time, allow them to do so–but do not let the other dogs harass them. Often, the new dog just needs time to relax and will come out to play on his own terms once he is feeling a bit more confident.

Be wary of the dogs who have no fear and come in ready to play. These dogs are often seen as the playful pet, perfect for off-leash play. In reality, these dogs are often over-stimulated and highly aroused. They are more likely to stumble into a fight than the more cautious dog who is taking the time to size up his new friends.

During new dog introductions, watch for stress signals and warning signs in the dogs (see chapters 4 and 5). Note stiffness, high tail carriage, and flattened ears. Watch the response of the other dogs in the group to the new dog. Sometimes the regular dog's reaction can be just as instructive as that of the new dog. For example, if you are using a dog who gets along with all dogs, but he is scared of the new dog, that is good information to consider as you conduct the introduction.

A dog who rudely approaches another dog without stopping to sniff will often be reprimanded by the other dog. This is to be expected, but still needs to be monitored. It is best not to let two dogs meet if either one is overly hyper or stimulated at the time of the meeting. Give them time to settle down before allowing them to meet.

Note the stiffness, high tail carriage, staring, and forward-leaning posture of the dog on left.

The dog on right is leaning forward with legs locked. The left dog has ears flattened back.

The following table outlines polite versus rude dog greeting behaviors.

Polite Greeting Behaviors	Rude Greeting Behaviors
• Indirect arcing approach • Relaxed body posture • Gently wagging tail • Averted eyes (soft or squinting) • Muzzle-to-face greeting, moving down body • Nose to rear circling • Equalizing body postures	• Direct head-on approach • Stiff legged posture • Stiff straight tail carriage • Direct staring • Muzzle over shoulders initially & holds • Not allowing rear sniffing • Jump on dog • Immediately barking in face

Sniffing the rear or genital area is an important part of dog greeting behavior. An appropriate rear sniff is mutual with relaxed postures and some distance between nose and rear. Time spent sniffing is mutually brief, generally lasting two to five seconds. In contrast, an inappropriate rear sniff is too close and pushy in proximity or the sniffing may last longer than five seconds.

MONITOR AFTER THE INTRODUCTION

The monitoring and assessment of a dog does not end once the dog is accepted into the group. Dog behavior is not static. You will see variations based on the time of day, the dogs in the group on any given day, the changes in environment at home, the changes in different staff members, etc. A dog's behavior can get worse in a playgroup. Make sure each dog is leaving the off-leash play session behaviorally better than when he arrived. Constant supervision is the key. Make notes of changes in behavior and be sure to keep the lines of communication with the dog owner open at all times.

Polite Greeting Behavior: Approaching in an arc

Polite Greeting Behavior: Relaxed bodies, equal body postures, dog on left has gentle tail wag

Rude Greeting Behavior: Jumping

Rude Greeting Behavior: Barking in face

Chapter 7 –
Effective Leadership

Our dogs require guidance. When we bring dogs into our homes, we have a responsibility to be a benevolent leader they can understand. This responsibility is magnified when, as pet professionals, we provide off-leash playgroups to dog owners. Effective and humane management, strong positive relationships, and sound leadership skills are the foundations of safe and fun off-leash playgroups.

Effective leadership cannot be provided by watching dogs play through a web- or video camera, a glass window, or by listening from the next room. Effective leadership can only be attained when you are physically present and supervising the dogs. Dog communication occurs through a series of dynamic, but subtle, body language signals and glances that appear flat when seen through a camera monitor. Once you hear a vocalization, interactions are likely to escalate more quickly than you can physically respond. Effective leadership is *proactive*, rather than *reactive,* intervention.

What is effective dog leadership? The dictionary defines a *leader* as a person who has commanding authority or influence. Think about bosses you enjoy working for or political leaders you respect. You can bet they shared the following traits of effective leaders:

- Earn the respect of followers through supportive, positive relationships
- Provide clear, consistent direction and feedback, and
- Support or protect followers in all situations.

To be an effective leader of dogs, you must have the same traits. The dogs must trust you and have a strong bond with you. Therefore, you must provide a strong foundation to build positive relationships, and provide clear guidance to the dogs. This ability has nothing to do with age or gender. A leader directs the operations, activities, or performance of the play without force or intimidation. In this chapter, we focus on the qualities that dogs need in their leaders and the tools used to provide leadership to the dogs. It is possible for the dogs to follow you because they *want to*, not because they have to.

~ Playgroups require supervision by trained attendants 100% of the time. This is not negotiable. If you are not willing to invest in the resources and training required to safely supervise dogs while they play, do not offer off-leash dog play services. ~

Leadership Self-Assessment			
	Rarely	Sometimes	Usually
1. Greetings with your dog are full of high energy and excitement.			
2. You get frustrated enforcing rules or boundaries with your dog.			
3. You raise your voice or yell to get your dog's attention.			
4. Your dog pulls on the leash when walking.			
5. When excited your dog does not respond to you.			
6. Your dog will run out an open door.			
7. You have to repeat commands several times before your dog responds.			
8. Your dog jumps up to greet you.			
9. Your dog is pushy and demanding for their meals and treats.			
10. You give your dog unlimited freedom and run of the house when at home.			

QUALITIES OF A LEADER

Effective leaders share the following key qualities:

1. Posture – walk tall with shoulders back and head held high
2. Attitude
    a. Calm
    b. Confident
    c. Decisive
    d. Quiet
3. Consistent in enforcing limits
4. Use of proactive intervention to prevent undesired behaviors

~ Effective leaders do not yell, scream, or intimidate their followers. They are not lazy or disengaged in the activities of their group. Effective leaders do not use physical force or punishment to accomplish their goals. ~

Your posture provides the dogs with a visual first impression. By walking tall, with head high, you are more likely to be viewed by the dogs as a leader. Keep your eyes focused above the dogs until you are ready to interact with them. Take time to allow all dogs to smell and sense your presence prior to interacting. Look at the dogs with a soft and inviting gaze, not a stare.

In addition to posture, you need a leader's attitude. We've all met individuals who seem to have a natural instinct that allows them to manage dogs easily. We call them "dog people" or say they are "good with dogs." A common attitude seems to be shared by these naturals. They have a peaceful attitude and rarely get ruffled or excited. They exude self-confidence and are often described as quiet. They tend to listen and observe groups rather than try to be the center of attention. Dogs are masters of nonverbal communication, and they sense these qualities.

POSTURE

The importance of posture is easy to test by using extremes to see different reactions. When you are with a group of dogs you don't know well, such as at a dog park, first walk among them slowly with slumped shoulders, head hung low, talking to each dog you meet (assume the posture of a victim).

After a brief period change to walking quickly with purpose, tall posture, shoulders back, head held high, ignoring dog greetings, constantly walking through the pack, and making them move out of your way instead of walking around them (assume the posture of royalty).

You should get a very different reaction from the dogs just from the change in your posture and movements.

Another quality of a good leader is consistency. Being consistent is one of your more challenging tasks. It is vital to set and consistently enforce limitations for the dogs. Like kids, dogs will push limits and quickly take advantage to exploit available opportunities. Effective leaders calmly and consistently enforce the rules of the group *every time* there is a violation. Inconsistency undermines your effectiveness.

Being consistent requires patience. You will be challenged daily, but it is important not to give in. Establishing rules upfront and training dogs to respond to them as they join the group is the easiest way to achieve consistency. It is much more difficult to introduce new rules or break bad habits after the dogs have been attending play sessions without them. If you feel frustrated, take a deep breath, review your training protocols, and try again. The key is to stay in control of the environment and remain calm. Remember, training takes time.

EFFECTIVE MANAGEMENT AT GATES

Consistently managing the dogs can be extremely effective. In this photo taken at K9 Capers in Agawam, Massachusetts, a group of dogs waits patiently at the *open* gate with eyes directed at daycare owner, Heather Staas, on the other side of the doorway. It is obvious doorway boundaries are consistently enforced. The dogs wait as a group for their cue to pass through the gate.

Good leaders are proactive and set their followers up to succeed. They learn each dog's history and limitations. They use positive reinforcement to reward behaviors they like. Proactive leaders seem to read dogs' minds. They interrupt or distract dogs before the dogs engage in unacceptable behavior. You will only be proactive if you learn to read and interpret canine body language as covered in the preceding chapters of this book.

~ Proactively set dogs up to succeed through effective use of time-outs when a dog is aroused and removal of dogs from the group in periods of high excitement. ~

EVENTS REQUIRING LEADERSHIP

During off-leash play sessions, just as in the family environment, certain key activities require more management and control. A dog's natural instincts and motivation in certain situations may cause the dog to become rowdier than usual. Lack of control by the staff at these times can easily lead to dangerous circumstances. Our challenge is to instill some self-control in the dogs during these triggering events. Some of these key events are listed below.

Instinct/Motivation	Family Events	Off-leash Playgroup Events
Search for resources	Daily walks	Approaching playgroup
Protect pack from danger	Strangers passing by house	Facility tours; strangers walking by playgroups
Reuniting with pack	Returning home from work	Dog entering playgroup during arrivals and after rest breaks

All of these are potentially energetic activities, especially when they occur in a group of dogs off-leash. You need to manage and control the interactions. In the home environment, this means your dogs should not drag you down the street on a walk. They should wait patiently for you to feed them. They should alert you to strangers approaching, but should not bark constantly once you have acknowledged the person. They should also wait politely for you to greet them when you arrive home. See appendix C for more information on these situations and how to handle them.

In off-leash dog playgroups, each event provides an opportunity for you to build a strong, positive relationship with the dogs in your care. Any time a dog on leash is walked in or out of the group, you should require loose-leash walking. This takes patience, but it's a great way to set the tone for good management and impulse control. Dogs learn loose-leash walking quickly when you are consistent.

LOOSE-LEASH WALKING AT PICK-UP TIMES

Managing the dogs at pick-up times was the first rule we implemented at Urban Tails doggie daycare in an effort to break bad habits that had developed. It took less than a week to retrain our dogs to walk on a loose leash by simply stopping anytime they pulled. The dogs soon learned that the only way to go forward was to keep the leash loose. Our clients were awed watching their former leash-puller walk politely. Our new rule was a great tool for training class referrals!

During play sessions, if dogs can see or hear people passing by, some dogs will bark. In your facility, this may happen when a client comes in or when street traffic passes by a play yard. You can acknowledge the alarm bark and teach a cue for the dogs to be quiet. This takes practice and must be trained with each dog who likes to bark. However, it will allow you to create a more peaceful environment and control the dog's arousal levels when unexpected visitors arrive.

New dogs joining the playgroup may cause high excitement. Control the excitement level by allowing new dogs to join the group only when all the dogs are calm and exhibiting self-control. Greet new arrivals only if they are calm. If they are demanding your attention by pawing or jumping on you, simply walk away or ignore them until they settle down. This can take time, but dogs who want to interact with you can learn that interaction only occurs when they are calm. Wait and greet the new dog when he is relaxed, calm, and has four feet on the floor.

High activity and energy also occurs when dogs depart from the group and during staff shift changes. Although necessary, these activities disrupt the existing group dynamic and cause excitement. It is important that you manage these events and keep excitement levels low by working with the dogs calmly and quietly using some of the leadership tools in this chapter.

TOOLS USED BY LEADERS
Key tools used by successful leaders include

1. Controlling resources
2. Utilizing basic obedience commands with rewards
3. Setting dogs up for success

Dogs are opportunists. They love to obtain and control resources such as food, toys, bedding, space, or even affection from people. Use these resources to your advantage using a "Nothing In Life Is Free (NILIF) program (see appendix C). By controlling these valuable items and offering them to the dogs on your schedule, you can help reinforce good behavior. Offer food to dogs only when they have earned it. Try not to mindlessly pet dogs who approach you. Pet and praise dogs when they are showing calm behavior such as sitting. Help the dogs understand physical boundaries by teaching dogs not to jump on you or crowd the doors or gates when you go through them. All interactive games between dogs and humans should be started and ended by you. In off-leash playgroups, controlling resources allows you to reinforce your leadership role without using force or intimidation.

CONTROLLING SPACE

Space can be one of the most valuable resources available in a playgroup. Establishing rules for managing space and teaching each dog the rules will make it much easier to run a safe play session.

BODY BLOCKING A JUMPING DOG

Anticipate the dog's behavior. As he approaches your space to jump on you, use your upper body and lean toward the dog. The body block can help to prevent the dog from jumping or can stop the dog after he has started jumping.

If the dog has a long history of jumping, an alternative method is to turn your back and ignore the dog completely, no eye contact, no touching, or even speaking to the dog. Once the dog shows respect for your space (all four feet are on the floor without leaning or pawing you) then—and only then--should you greet them. By controlling the space around your body, you gain control of the dog.

Make sure the dogs respect your personal space. Good leaders wait for the dog to behave politely before petting them. Avoid petting dogs when they are demonstrating rude behavior, such as jumping up, leaning on you, or demanding attention by pawing or barking. The look-away is a useful tool to discourage these attention-seeking behaviors. Turn your head to the side with chin up and move your eyes away from the dog. If the dog moves to make eye contact with you, continue the look-away. This can be an effective way to teach dogs that rude behavior does not work to get attention.

Body blocking can be used to maintain physical space in a dog group. Dogs are much more space sensitive than people. Leaning your body slightly forward or backward is readily noticed by dogs and can change their movement.

When using your body to communicate, lean in the opposite direction you want the dog to go. Leaning toward the dog will cause him to back away from you (this works best if you cross your arms so your hands do not accidentally pet or encourage the dog). Leaning away from the dog will encourage him to come closer. Play around with this; it's a very powerful communication tool.

You will need to carefully manage the space around the play area's doorway. This entry and exit area should have a defined perimeter of space around it (2-3 feet). Dogs learn they get to play when they go through the door. This causes very high excitement levels around doorways. Dogs can be taught to wait at a doorway, but it takes practice and continual rehearsal.

Controlling space can also involve managing height. An increase in height can sometimes equate to an increase in social status. Ever try to sit on the floor with your dog? Many dogs will take this gesture as an invitation to play and will jump on you to engage in a little fun. In an off-leash setting, this activity can be dangerous to humans and should be avoided. Also, small dogs should not be picked up and carried in a playgroup since this will sometimes cause other dogs to jump and nip at them.

SPACE MANAGEMENT WITH SMALLER DOGS

With smaller dogs, you can extend your personal space without bending over. In this photo taken at Miss Daisy's Dog Camp, a small-dog-only facility in Tomball, Texas, owner, Debbie Oliver, uses a tennis ball launcher as an extension of her arm to control the space around her. By extending the ball launcher—never to swing at, scare, or hit the dogs—you can keep the dogs from crowding you. This often works much better with smaller dogs than leaning down or bending over to move them since those behaviors generally encourage the dogs to approach you.

To introduce space rules to an established group of dogs, start with two or three dogs at a time. Effectively managing a group takes work, but your payoff is an easy-to-handle, safe, and fun playgroup.

CONTROLLING OTHER RESOURCES

The leader controls games and toys in a playgroup. You should be the one to start and stop interactive games between humans and dogs, such as playing fetch and blowing bubbles. You also decide when toys are allowed and when to remove them. Toys should only be allowed when the dogs play nicely as a group with them. Remember that toys can be viewed as valuable resources and can trigger inappropriate resource guarding behavior. It is important to recognize this and remove either the dog or the toys from the group.

Dogs may see items as a resource when we see nothing of value. The dog gets to decide what is valuable. Some dogs guard water bowls, an area of space, and even dog poop! Dogs may resource guard their owners or staff members in the group. For more information on resource guarding, see chapter 5.

Play equipment, chairs, beds, or couches are common in dog play areas. Ideally, you should be able to call each dog off them. The dogs should also be willing to move if you approach the item to claim the space. It is never acceptable for a dog to warn you away from a position of height by growling or snapping. If this is happening, the dog is a threat to your staff and requires training to become an acceptable playgroup member.

USING BASIC OBEDIENCE COMMANDS

Using basic obedience commands allows you to communicate more effectively with the dogs and will help you be a better leader by building strong, positive relationships with them. Positive reinforcement is an excellent method of training. However, it can be risky to use food rewards in a group setting. Instead, use other rewards such as verbal praise, toys, and physical attention. Be sure to give lots of reinforcement when dogs respond appropriately to your commands.

Teach the come command to each dog to help with your management of the group. Being able to call a dog away from other dogs or people is useful in redirecting the dog or interrupting an escalation that is getting out of hand. It is an excellent tool and should be practiced daily with every dog in the group. Practicing come with the dogs during low-energy play helps you get fast responses when you really need them.

Other commands needed in managing playgroups are sit, wait, leave it, and off. Make sure your entire staff knows what commands you use and the definitions of each. Dogs are not robots. They will work for whoever is consistent with them. Each of your staff members will need to practice with the dogs. Using obedience commands during games is a great way to reinforce your position and build a strong relationship with the dogs. For instance, have the dogs sit as a group prior to throwing the ball. This requires self-control and focuses their attention on you. Anytime a dog starts to get highly excited or aroused, use obedience commands to give him an alternative behavior. This shifts his mental energy and sets the dog up for success. For more information on teaching obedience commands, see the resources located in appendix D.

SETTING DOGS UP FOR SUCCESS

Your job is to protect and manage the dogs in your care. You must know each dog well enough to help him avoid situations he cannot handle. Observe each dog's body language so you can intervene before a serious incident. Keep arousal levels low by managing the level and type of play in the group. A reliable come and other obedience commands will give you control to help you do this. Good leaders set the dogs up for success. They are proactive and intervene prior to problem behaviors occurring.

RECOGNIZING EFFECTIVE LEADERSHIP

How do you recognize effective dog leadership? Leaders have the ability to control, direct, and inhibit behaviors of dogs in the group without force or intimidation. They can move a dog away from a resource without yelling or manhandling the dog. Dogs want to follow them and do so willingly.

Off-leash playgroups managed by an effective leader have a sense of harmony and are relatively quiet. Respectful leaders produce respectful followers. Dog body postures are relaxed, and you rarely see signs of stress. There is balanced play between the dogs and arousal levels remain low. The dogs are having fun and the leader is relaxed, but attentive.

Your leadership skills need improvement if you:

1. Yell to get the attention of the dogs
2. Yell to verbally reprimand the dogs
3. Keep correction tools (e.g., spray bottles, shake cans, etc) near you at all times and use them frequently
4. Have a lot of dogs going to time out
5. Have play arousal levels escalate frequently
6. Have frequent dog-to-dog altercations and/or injuries
7. Cannot call each dog to you with ease
8. Cannot control behavior of most dogs at gates or doorways
9. Cannot walk most dogs on a loose leash
10. Have a lot of barking throughout the day

If you find you need some brushing up on your leadership skills, take heart! Leadership skills can improve. The first step in this process is to honestly assess where you fall short. The second step is to make a commitment to work daily at improving your skills. The third and most important step is to believe that you can be an effective leader!

Look back to the Leadership Self-Assessment you completed earlier in this chapter. Score your responses to find the strength of your dog leadership skills. Assign 3 points for each Usually answer, 2 points for each Sometimes, and 1 point for each Rarely. Total your score and compare it to the following chart.

Score	Leadership Effectiveness
10 – 15	Very Effective – congratulations you have a great base for managing off-leash dog play-groups. Continue to practice your skills to perfect them.
16 – 20	Good Skills – focus on identifying weak areas and reading those sections again for ways to be an effective leader of off-leash playgroups.
21 – 25	Work in Progress – study this chapter and implement the suggestions with your own dog. You'll see that the skills transfer to managing off-leash playgroups.
26 - 30	Believe It – study this chapter and read the leadership references listed in appendix D. You can gain the leader skills needed to manage off-leash dog playgroups.

Look at the specific questions on Leadership Self-Assessment and use the chart below to identify areas of focus.

Questions	Leadership Area of Focus
1 - 3	Qualities – Review the qualities of leadership and work to stay calm, take deep breaths, and smile. Also focus on staying consistent with your rules and boundaries. Implement a "no yelling" policy, but keep your tone of voice firm. This is an area where success breeds more success and helps your confidence grow.
4 – 5	Events – Review the events where leadership is required with dogs. During these times, focus on consistency in asserting your leadership position without force and intimidation. Stay in control of the situation and reward the dogs when they respond appropriately.
6 - 10	Tools – Obedience training is a key tool in asserting your leadership and should be fun for you and your dogs. Incorporate commands into your daily interactions, such as having them sit prior to eating or getting a treat and be sure to reward frequently for good behavior. Consider the NILIF method (see appendix C) as a way to get started. Be sure that you have defined rules and boundaries and are consistent in enforcing them.

Effective leadership is a foundation for safe management of off-leash playgroups. It is something you must work on every day and in every interaction with dogs. Master effective dog leadership skills, and you will enjoy off-leash playgroups almost as much as the dogs do!

Chapter 8 –
Controlling the Group

STAFF RESPONSIBILITY

Your clients have entrusted the care of their very special dogs to you. For that reason, your top priority must be to keep the dogs safe while they play at your facility. Proper training of employees and written dog-handling policies are important aspects of a safe off-leash playgroup environment.

Chapter 7 covered the important aspects of effective leadership in a playgroup. Good leadership in an off-leash environment is vital. With proper management, many problems will be averted before they start. When dogs do display inappropriate behavior, effective leadership is required to prevent these behaviors from escalating. In addition, any control measures, discussed in this chapter, will be easier to implement if the people have formed a strong relationship with the dogs in their care. With that in mind, this chapter addresses the management options most often used to control groups of dogs playing off leash.

PLAY AREA ACTIVITY LEVEL

Remember: the greater the activity in the play area, the greater the potential for a fight. For this reason, discourage horseplay and exuberant activity by people attending the play session. Such activity will only heighten the dogs' overall state of arousal and increase the potential for problems. Your job is to monitor the dogs' activity, but not create unruly play between the dogs. Human interaction with the dogs needs to be calm and controlled.

INTERACTIONS BETWEEN DOGS AND PEOPLE

Forming strong social bonds with people is an important part of a dog's behavioral development. Conflicts between people and dogs often occur when each other's signals are misunderstood. We have a responsibility to learn and use the language our dogs understand. We need to remember that, quite simply, our dog is a dog, and not a human family member. Chapter 1 describes the basics of understanding canine body language.

There are two common mistakes people make in communicating with dogs. The first is in our greeting approach. We often greet dogs the same way we would greet another person. We give a big friendly smile, reach out our hand, and lean toward the dog. In dog language, our smile resembles a snarl, the outstretched hand invades their personal space, and leaning over them can be perceived as a threat. From the dog's point of view, this greeting is not friendly and will threaten fearful and less-confident dogs.

The second common communication mistake is to hug our dogs. For us, this is a natural and comfortable expression of friendship and caring. In dog language, hugging can be perceived as a threatening gesture. At best, some dogs will tolerate the hug. However, many will try to avoid or prevent the hug through the use of aggression. It is our responsibility to know and teach human interactions that are friendly in dog language.

Human and Dog Greetings

It is not enough to have good intentions when meeting a new dog. We must also adjust our greeting behaviors to appear friendly to the dog. Dogs use their nose and mouth to explore their world while we use our eyes and hands. When greeting dogs, keep your eye and hand contact to a minimum. This will reduce fear in the dog and allow you to make friends more quickly.

The following greeting sequence is perceived as friendly and polite by a dog:

- Squat down and turn your body sideways to the dog, arms near body
- Look away to be seen as non-threatening
- Wait until the dog comes to you for a sniff
- If the dog is nervous, make champing noises and blink your eyes
- Once the dog sniffs you, stand up slowly; your height will no longer be as frightening
- With a fearful dog, it is often best to totally ignore him until he is more comfortable in the surroundings

---

GREETING A GROUP OF OFF-LEASH DOGS

Crista Meyer of Urban Tails in Houston, Texas shared her method of greeting dogs in an off-leash setting. When new dogs join the playgroup, walk or stand with arms at your side, but your palms exposed. Dogs will come and bump your palms in a greeting, similar to a face lick or neck nudge. If allowed to greet in this way, the dog will usually wander off after the greeting. There is less excitement and jumping in the greeting ceremony if you use this approach when you enter an established playgroup.

HANDLING AND MOVING DOGS

You will often need to move dogs away from the gate in order to get another dog through. You might have to move a dog into a crate. You may have to handle a dog to take off or put on a collar or leash. However, no matter why you are handling the dog, you and your staff need to be careful when doing so.

Rapidly grabbing a dog's collar is a bad idea. A dog may be startled or even snap if suddenly grabbed by the collar. Instead, use a slip-lead that can be put over the dog's head and around the neck to move the dog. Keep a slip-lead readily available at all times.

COLLARS OR NO COLLARS

You need to decide whether or not you want the dogs in your playgroups to wear collars. Carrying a slip-lead will allow you to move the dogs safely if you are not using collars.

Collars can be dangerous because a dog can get his jaw stuck in another dog's collar. If this is a risk in your facility, ensure you have easy access to strong scissors that can quickly cut through a dog's collar.

If you must use collars for identification of the dogs, consider using a break-away collar. These collars are designed to unhook if they are snagged on something. Keep in mind that these collars are not useful if you try to move a dog by the collar because the collar will unhook when you grab it.

Metal and heavy leather collars of any kind are dangerous in a playgroup and need to be removed before allowing the dog to attend.

Also, avoid pushing dogs into each other while moving them. Just like people, dogs have varying spatial needs. Some dogs require more space around them than others. Pushing one dog against a dog who requires more space may result in a fight.

ROOM SETUP

The setup of a play area can dramatically help in the management of the group of dogs playing off leash. The right amount of space will help give the dogs room to get away from one another without overcrowding. Generally speaking, you can estimate a space requirement of 50 to 100 square feet of play area space per dog, depending on the size of the dog. This is a good way to estimate how many dogs you can take in your playgroup and allows you to estimate a cost per dog that is feasible for your facility as well.

STAFFING AND SPACE REQUIREMENTS

A playgroup session should be staffed at a ratio of one person to every 10-15 dogs, depending on the size of the dogs and the experience of the person. Remember that you can teach owners to act as staff members if they attend social playgroups with their dog.

For the safest play, estimate 50 to 100 square feet per dog, depending on the size of the dog.

PLAYGROUND EQUIPMENT AND TOYS

In an off-leash play setting, dogs generally play more with one another than with toys. However, they do enjoy having some fun things to climb and playthings to chew. Avoid using vinyl and latex toys because these toys can be easily ripped apart and possibly ingested. Hard rubber toys are a better choice.

Special playground equipment, designed especially for dogs, is very durable in an off-leash environment and gives your facility a bright, colorful appearance. Anything the dogs can climb needs to be an appropriate size for the dogs. Small dogs can easily fall or jump off large slides. Even for larger dogs, it is best to avoid play equipment higher than 3 feet. Dog agility equipment, such as tires, tunnels, or jumps, may be used. However, keep all jump heights low to prevent injury to the dogs.

Playground equipment and pool for the dogs

If you run short playgroups and you do not have space for playground equipment, the dogs will still have fun. However, at a minimum you should place chairs, small tables, or crates around the room so the dogs have access to get under or in things if they are feeling overwhelmed. It is important to give the dogs a safe haven where they can retreat if they feel it necessary to do so.

Give dogs places where they can retreat.

Fun Toys for the Dogs

Agility Equipment	Rope Toys
Indestructible Ball	Small Plastic Pool
KONG® Toys	Squiggly Wiggly Ball
Nylabone® Products	Tennis Balls
Playground Equipment	Tug Toys

TOY SAFETY

Remember to check toys frequently for wear and tear. Throw away toys that are fraying, breaking, or crumbling. Replace tennis balls that become soft. Ensure the toy size is adequate for the dogs playing with them. Toys that are too small can be choking hazards for larger dogs. Avoid toys that can be chewed apart easily because these can be ingested by dogs and cause an intestinal blockage. If you use toys in your playgroup, be aware of the signs of resource guarding behaviors (see chapter 5).

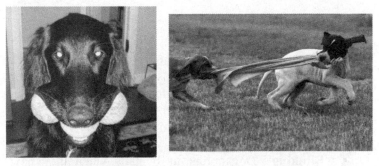

Dogs enjoy balls and playing tug games.

GAMES TO PLAY

The list below contains games and activities you and your staff can use in an off-leash setting. Note that any games that increase arousal levels or create potential resource guarding situations should be moderated.

- Find the person – have a staff member hide and encourage the dogs to find him. (Initially, the staff member may need to call the dogs to help them understand the game)
- Follow the leader – the dogs will enjoy following you around the facility with a little encouragement from you
- Fetch – allowing dogs to chase toys or balls can be fun if the dogs will not fight over the objects
- Chasing bubbles – many dogs love to follow bubbles blown into the air
- Tug – play this game with dogs once they know a strong leave it command
- Obedience commands – practice sit, stay, off, come and other obedience commands frequently

---

READING BODY LANGUAGE

It's vital that everyone supervising the dogs understands canine body language as discussed in chapters 1-5. In particular, chapter 2 discussed common social gestures used by dogs. The list below highlights some of the gestures commonly used by dogs toward humans:

- **Blinking–** Dogs blink at humans when they have been too harsh or seem mean or angry.
- **Displacement Activity–**Shown in situations where dogs feel pressure to solve a problem they don't understand and when corrected or reprimanded. They may try to escape or pick up and carry objects to avoid the uncomfortable situation.

- **Hip Nudge**–Dogs typically use this as a signal of friendliness when greeting people. The dog will walk toward someone and then turn around and nudge gently with the hip or rear end.
- **Leaning**–Dogs often lean their weight in a display of confidence.
- **Pawing**–Pawing in the air may signal frustration from not understanding a person's request. Pawing is a pacifying gesture. Pawing that includes touching the person's leg or hand is an attention-seeking gesture.
- **Smile**–Some dogs smile in a manner that resembles a human smile: mouth is open, lips drawn back, and teeth are visible. The rest of the dog's body language will help you differentiate a smile from a snarl. It is a pacifying gesture that is reserved for people, usually those they know. It is seldom used toward other dogs.
- **Yawn**–dogs will yawn to show friendliness as a pacifying behavior. After a scolding or a training behavior that makes them feel insecure, yawning is a displacement behavior or a stress signal.

People can converse a little with dogs using their language, though we will never be fluent because our bodies and faces are too different from dogs'. We can portray a confident and tall body posture to gain trust and respect. When a dog is nervous, we can squat, turn sideways, and display pacifying gestures to provide comfort. Focus on visual signals sent with your body posture, weight shifts, and facial expressions more than on your tone of voice to communicate most effectively with dogs.

~ Grabbing dogs by the scruff, rolling them on their backs, or pulling them by the jowls is simply unnecessary if your playgroup is properly screened and managed. These methods are not only scary to the dogs, they are also unsafe for the staff. ~

CONTROLLING INAPPROPRIATE BEHAVIOR

Several methods to control inappropriate behavior can be useful with dogs playing off leash. Not all methods will work for every dog. Experiment to see what is most useful for each situation and each dog.

Strive to control behavior by using a positive approach to intervention. Usually, interrupting the dogs will end most undesirable behavior and allow you to redirect their behavior to more appropriate play. In some cases, giving a dog a brief timeout in a crate will help to settle him down enough that he will play more appropriately. Work together with the dog owners to resolve any issues concerning dogs playing and be sure to inform the clients of any discipline used with their dogs.

This chapter outlines some of the most commonly used, safe methods for controlling dogs playing off leash. The vast majority of problems in an off-leash playgroup can be resolved using proper leadership and redirection. There is very little need for other measures of control if you are properly screening and supervising the dogs in your care.

There is no reason to use physical methods of punishment. Therefore, we do not cover any methods of control that use harsh or physical methods. Grabbing dogs by the scruff, rolling them on their backs, or pulling them by their jowls is simply unnecessary if your playgroup is properly screened and managed. These methods are not only scary to the dogs, they are also unsafe for the staff.

Rest Periods

Off-leash play sessions should always include mandatory rest periods for the dogs. A rule of thumb is to spend one-third of the session allowing the dogs to play with one another, one-third of the time as structured training sessions or games, and the final third should be a rest period for the dogs. The rest period will give the dogs a much-needed break and it also gives your staff a break from supervising the dogs. For example: in a short playgroup (45-60 minutes), have the owners take the dogs outside for a 5- to 10-minute potty break; in a daycare setting, crate the dogs for a 1- to 2-hour naptime. These break periods are critical to maintaining stress-free, calm dogs in your playgroup. Too much uninterrupted play or a free-for-all environment creates too much arousal and does not help teach dogs any impulse control.

MUZZLES IN DAYCARE

Generally, muzzles are not appropriate for playgroups unless you are specifically working on behavior modification and *all* the owners agree to this idea. Muzzles used to prevent barking may restrict panting and can cause a dog to overheat. Muzzles used to prevent aggression toward people or dogs, if not used with proper training techniques, can cause frustration in a dog and can cause his aggressive behavior to become worse. In addition, most clients bringing their dog to a playgroup session will be noticeably alarmed if they see a dog wearing a muzzle.

Redirecting the Dog (Splitting)

Redirecting the dog will often control undesirable behavior by changing the context of the dog's play. Simply walking near two dogs playing, calling their names in a high happy tone, or acting silly will usually distract most dogs. This method is the primary means of controlling the dogs in a playgroup. When redirecting the dogs, the goal is to remain happy and upbeat, not angry.

Calling Timeouts

Timeouts can help deter inappropriate behavior. If a dog is displaying inappropriate behavior, such as barking at another dog, say "timeout" and gently lead the dog to a crate. Set a timer for 30-60 seconds and then allow the dog to return to the play area. Repeat this sequence for any specific behavior, such as barking, that you would like to deter in an individual dog. Teach your staff to use the timeout effectively. The timeout is not meant to be a place to put the dog when your staff is frustrated. Instead, the timeout is meant to be a structured tool used for safety and training.

Note that the method described above can help teach dogs how to behave properly. The timeout marker (saying "timeout") and the act of leading the dog to the crate must occur immediately (within 1-2 seconds) of the offending behavior. This method will not work as a training tool if the timing is not correct. However, crates can still be useful to give dogs a rest break and help reduce arousal level in the room.

Using a Leash or Collar

Some over-stimulated dogs relax when a staff member puts a leash on the dog and takes him for a low-key walk around the room. The leash is being used simply to calm the dog down, not to correct the dog physically. Additionally, a Gentle Leader® headcollar has a calming effect on many dogs. The collar, when worn properly, still allows the dog to open his mouth, eat, and drink, but it also helps to settle him down. Dogs wearing a Gentle Leader or leash must be supervised to ensure they do not chew or get tangled in them.

Spraying with Water

For some dogs, a stream of water sprayed in their face serves as a deterrent to inappropriate behavior such as jumping or barking. As with any direct punishment applied to a dog, it must be applied immediately (within 1-2 seconds of the undesirable behavior occurring) and should be effective within four to five tries on a dog. If a dog is sprayed with water more than five times and the inappropriate behavior continues, then the water is not effective and should stop.

Although spraying with water can be useful in a playgroup setting for some dogs, it is easy for the staff to overuse this punitive method. Spraying a dog with water should be a last-resort measure to try if redirecting the dog, giving a timeout, and using a leash have already been tried. It is not meant as a replacement for other methods.

A WORD ABOUT CORRECTIONS

When dealing with inappropriate behavior in dogs, ensure you do not inadvertently correct a dog who is not doing anything wrong. For instance, making loud noises (yelling, throw objects, shaking cans with pennies, etc.) to discourage one dog from inappropriate behavior affects all the dogs in the play area. This type of group punishment should not be used unless absolutely necessary (for instance, in the event of a fight). It is unfair to the non-offending dogs in the room.

Physical punishment of the dogs, such as rolling dogs on their back, grabbing them by the scruff of the neck, or pinning them on the ground, should not be used because this teaches the dogs to be wary of the people supervising the group. These methods also put you at high risk of being bitten because dogs often defend themselves when being handled in this manner.

If you have employees, set a good example for them. Employees will imitate each other. However, the fact that one person is able to safely roll a dog on his back does not mean a new employee will be able to do so. There is a huge liability for you, as the owner of a facility, if you allow your staff to operate this way.

Any use of punishment needs to be carefully monitored. The staff needs to keep an eye on their emotions and frustration level to ensure the dogs are not being punished excessively or unfairly. Clients need to be aware of any discipline used with the dogs. Most punishment can be avoided by simply teaching your staff to be proactive and redirecting behavior as early as possible.

Using a Citronella Collar

A citronella collar is a small mechanical device worn around a dog's neck. If a dog barks, the citronella collar emits a puff of citronella spray in the dog's face. For many dogs, this is a strong deterrent against barking. The citronella collar can be useful with some dogs in a playgroup. However, there are some drawbacks in an off-leash setting. Dogs who are strongly engaged in the barking behavior due to fear or anxiety will usually not respond to the citronella. They will continue barking despite the spray in their face. Do not use the citronella collar for these dogs because it is not effective. In addition, in an off-leash setting, the collar will sometimes go off if a dog near the one wearing the collar barks. This is unfair to the dog with the citronella collar on. The use of the citronella collar should only be considered as a last-resort measure.

For information on controlling a group of dogs if a fight occurs, see chapter 5.

Putting it All Together

The basics outlined in this book are key to effective management of off-leash playgroups. This is where the management traffic signal guides listed throughout the book will help. A series of green signals with one yellow is a low-level concern. You can allow the interactions to proceed. A series of yellow signals with a red signal is of greater concern. These interactions should be interrupted and may require removal of a dog from the playgroup, either temporarily or permanently.

Play behavior that is fun and safe between two individual dogs could quickly turn to conflict in another pair. It is our responsibility as pet professionals to learn and know the difference. Understanding dog language, effective leadership, and proper management of a group of off-leash dogs will allow you to run fun playgroups and keep the dogs safe.

Appendix A –
Emotional States

Learning to quickly read and interpret dogs' emotional states and then predict their actions can be challenging at first. We have used the management traffic signal symbols to help you filter the information.

Initially, try to focus on whether a given action would be classified as green, yellow, or red. Once you are comfortable with these designations, start to look at combinations of signals. The five primary aspects you'll be focusing on are

- Posture and movement
- Ears
- Tail
- Facial expression
- Vocalization

Think of each of these as a word, which in combination with the others forms a sentence. What is each dog saying?

The following pages include detailed charts and annotated photos of dogs displaying various emotional states to help you become more comfortable understanding the dogs in your off-leash playgroup.

Green

Emotional State	Posture & Movement	Ears	Tail	Facial Expression	Vocalization
Neutral & Relaxed	Balanced Relaxed Loose & curvy	Natural for dog Loose & relaxed	Natural for dog Lower than horizontal Loose & relaxed	Soft eyes Mouth relaxed & open slightly	None
Curious, Eager, or Excited	Normal Possible wiggle or stand tip-toe	Perked up Forward	Up Fast, small wags	Wide eyes Mouth open Teeth covered Possible panting	Short bark, "ruff" Whining
Friendly	Normal Stands still or rear end wiggling	Perked up	Up or out from body Small wags	Wide open eyes, alert Mouth relaxed & slightly open	High-pitch bark Short bark Champing
Playful or Happy	Relaxed Play-bow Excited bouncing, circling	Perked up Forward Relaxed	Wagging Large circle wagging	Wide open eyes, sparkling Mouth relaxed & open slightly Teeth covered Panting	High-pitch barking Play growling

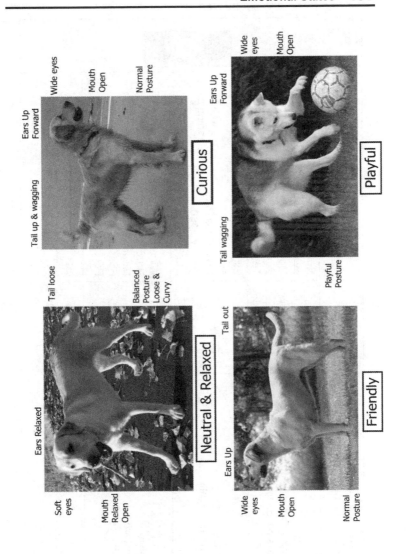

Curious

Ears Up Forward
Wide eyes
Mouth Open
Normal Posture
Tail up & wagging

Playful

Ears Up Forward
Wide eyes
Mouth Open
Tail wagging
Playful Posture

Neutral & Relaxed

Tail loose
Balanced Posture Loose & Curvy
Ears Relaxed
Soft eyes
Mouth Relaxed Open

Friendly

Tail out
Ears Up
Wide eyes
Mouth Open
Normal Posture

Emotional State	Posture & Movement	Ears	Tail	Facial Expression	Vocalization
Alert	Normal Slightly forward Possibly on tiptoe	Up Turning to hear sounds	Up Possible slow wag	Normal-to-wide open eyes Mouth closed or slightly open Teeth covered	None Rapid alarm bark Low whine
Anxious	Tense Lowered slightly	Partially back	Partially lowered	Slightly narrowed eyes Mouth closed or slightly open Lips pulled back	Low whine Moaning bark
Aroused	Tense Forward Stiff legs	Up Forward	Up Bristled Stiff wag	Wide open eyes Hard staring Mouth tense Possible lifted lips Possible panting	Rapid bark

Continued on next page

Emotional State	Posture & Movement	Ears	Tail	Facial Expression	Vocalization
Chase (beginning stage)	Tense Crouched low Legs bent to run	Up Forward	Extends straight out from body	Wide open eyes, alert Mouth slightly open Excited panting	None
Confident	Tall Hackles may rise	Up Forward	Up or straight out Stiff & full	Wide open eyes Staring Mouth closed or slightly open	Low growl
Fearful	Tense Crouched Shivering or trembling	Low on head Flattened	Between legs	Narrow eyes, averted Possible half-moon eye Lips drawn back Teeth showing	Low yelp, whine, growl, bark, or scream
Subordinate (low rank)	Low Paw lift Lies on back, belly up	Low on head Flattened	Between legs	Narrowed slit eyes Possible half-moon eye Lips drawn back Teeth showing Face licking	None Low whining or whimper

Anxious

Eyes Slightly Narrowed
Mouth Closed Lips Back
Ears Partially Back
Tail Lowered
Tense Posture Lowered

Chase

Wide eyes
Mouth Open
Ears Up Forward
Tail Extended Out
Tense Crouched Posture

Alert

Wide Eyes
Mouth Closed
Ears Up Turning
Tail - not typical, may rise & wag slowly
Normal Posture Forward

Aroused

Ears Up Forward
Wide Eyes Staring
Tail Up
Posture Forward

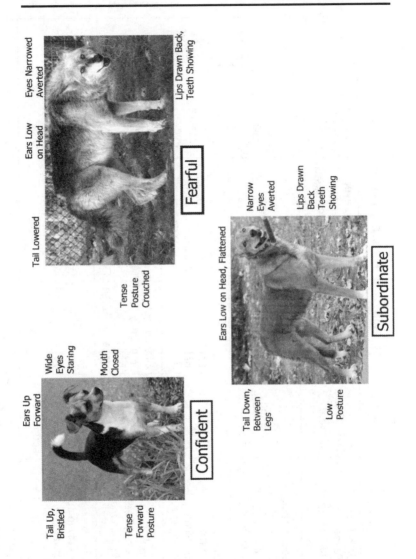

Fearful

Eyes Narrowed Averted

Lips Drawn Back, Teeth Showing

Ears Low on Head

Tail Lowered

Tense Posture Crouched

Subordinate

Narrow Eyes Averted

Lips Drawn Back Teeth Showing

Ears Low on Head, Flattened

Tail Down, Between Legs

Low Posture

Confident

Wide Eyes Staring

Mouth Closed

Ears Up Forward

Tail Up, Bristled

Tense Forward Posture

Emotional State	Posture & Movement	Ears	Tail	Facial Expression	Vocalization
Aggression, offensive	Up & forward Tense Hackles up on neck	Up Forward	Straight out from body Fluffed Stiff slow wag	Hard staring eyes Snarl or C-shaped lips drawn forward Teeth showing	Snarling Long deep growl Loud bark
Aggression, defensive	Low & back Tense Hackles up on back & tail	Flattened	Very low or between legs	Narrow eyes Possible ½-moon eye Lips pulled back Teeth & gums show Wrinkled muzzle	Snarling Growl-bark
Flight (beginning stage)	Low Tense Shivering Ready to run	Back	Low or between legs	Wide open eyes Possible ½-moon eye Mouth slightly open Possible drooling	None Possible whine
Guarding	Up Tense, freezes Hackles may rise	Up. Forward	Straight out from body Rigid Possible fluffed	Wide open, alert Mouth slightly open Teeth showing Possible snapping	Loud bark Growl Snarl
Predatory	Low Ready to spring forward Rigid May sniff air	Alert Forward or back to catch sounds	Low Straight out	Wide open staring eyes, focused Mouth closed	None

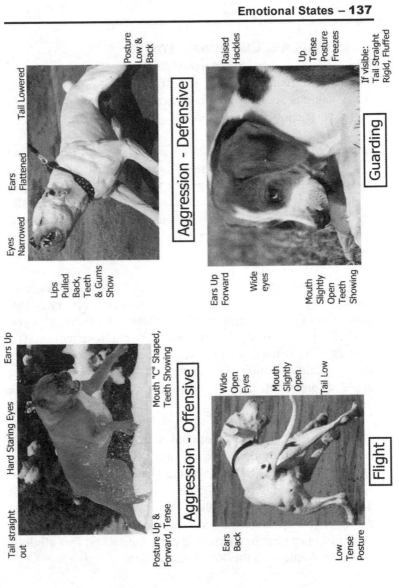

Aggression – Defensive

Eyes Narrowed

Ears Flattened

Tail Lowered

Posture Low & Back

Lips Pulled Back, Teeth & Gums Show

Guarding

Raised Hackles

Up Tense Posture Freezes

If visible: Tail Straight Rigid, Fluffed

Ears Up Forward

Wide eyes

Mouth Slightly Open Teeth Showing

Aggression – Offensive

Tail straight out

Hard Staring Eyes

Ears Up

Mouth "C" Shaped, Teeth Showing

Posture Up & Forward, Tense

Flight

Wide Open Eyes

Mouth Slightly Open

Tail Low

Ears Back

Low Tense Posture

RANK ORDER & EMOTIONAL STATES

The following chart summarizes the scale of rank order and canine emotional states. The off-leash play management traffic signals are included to illustrate the areas on the scale that require caution and action.

Start in the middle of the chart with the neutral posture and work your way toward the behavioral extremes. Surrounding the neutral dog body language are the other emotional states that are classified as green: curious, eager, excited, friendly, happy, and playful. The body language associated with these emotions are similar to the neutral posture and on the scale would be near the center.

As you move up from the center, the postures increase in confidence; as you move down the postures reflect a less confident or inferior rank. Both of these directions take you to behaviors classified with yellow management traffic signals. You'll need to observe the dogs closely to be sure that you and the other dogs in the playgroup are reading the dog's expressions properly and dogs remain comfortable interacting.

Moving to the left, the emotional states progress to aggression. The aroused, alert, anxious, and chase states are yellow on our management traffic signal as they can quickly result in aggression. Moving to the right, these same states in different dogs or situations can result in fear. When you see any of these yellow postures or states, monitor the interactions carefully to ensure they remain a part of play and that all dogs are comfortable with the social interaction.

As discussed in the body language chapter, the extreme postures of aggression and fear are not common in off-leash playgroups. The other states of guarding, flight, and predation are definite red signals that require you to intervene immediately to avoid conflict between dogs.

Dog Body Language: Rank Order & Emotional States

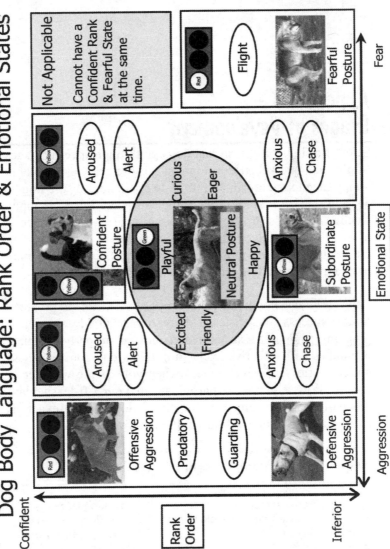

In off-leash playgroups, your goal is to keep rank order and emotional states as close as possible to those in the middle circle. This translates to healthy, fun play for the dogs.

Appendix B -
Stages of Development

Scientific studies confirm that dogs go through specific stages of physical and social development. These critical periods in puppy development can affect the temperament of the dog as an adult. These studies also indicate that once a puppy reaches 4 months of age, he has either made—or not made—most of the social connections he will ever make. During critical periods, a seemingly insignificant experience may have a great impact on later behavior.

This early development is an important factor in a dog's future success in off-leash playgroups. Off-leash puppy programs should be structured to ensure properly matched playmates with effective leadership. Be sure to consider these critical periods of development when you decide whether or not to allow a puppy to participate in your off-leash playgroup. The ages outlined in the chart below are not exact, as breed and size of dog will affect the timeframe.

Stage	Key Developments	Playgroup Considerations
Neonatal (birth to 2 weeks)	Devoted to obtaining nutrition. Senses: touch & taste (eyes closed & deaf); reacts to cold & pain. Slow crawl. Vocalization: distress calls	Too young for playgroup. Puppies can be harmed physically more than psychologically.
Transition (2-3 weeks)	Changes in basic sensory & motor capabilities. Period begins with eyes opening & ends when sounds cause a startle response. Teeth form. Begin to see adult behaviors, movements & nutrition.	Too young for playgroup. Puppies begin to show communication through body language.

Stage	Key Developments	Playgroup Considerations
Awareness (3-4 weeks)	First uses senses of sight & hearing. Key period of development so puppy should be kept stable & not moved. Develops comfort from the "familiar."	Too young for playgroup. Puppies begin to learn what it is to be a dog.
Canine Socialization (1-2 months)	Critical period for psychological development/damage; social & location relationships are important. New behavior patterns related to mother & littermates; puppy investigates. Weaning to solid food with eliminations outside nest box. Adult behaviors in playful form, social play, develops relationships easily, tail wag begins.	Too young for playgroup. Learns to use body language & vocalizations to communicate. Learns to accept discipline from mother. Social bonding with humans & others. Key time to be with litter to learn dog language; stay with mother & litter at least through 7 weeks.
Human socialization (2-3 months)	Good time to introduce puppy to new home & environment. Attention span is short & learning is permanent. Fear response to strangers.	Puppy socialization in small groups with properly matched puppy & adult dog playmates. Begin positive puppy training.
Fear Impact Period 1 (2-3 months)	Any traumatic experience may have a lasting impression on puppy. New experiences must be non-threatening. Take extra care to make puppy feel safe.	Critical that all social interactions be fun & positive. Fearful adult behaviors can result from experiences puppy perceives as threatening.
Seniority Classification (3-4 months)	Period of adjustment, all sense organs fully developed. Permanent teeth growing; results in chewing & biting behaviors. May begin to experiment with some aggressive behaviors, if confident.	Playgroups with effective management and leadership. Discourage all biting behaviors. Consistent enforcement of rules & boundaries with a lot of patience and positive reinforcement.

Stage	Key Developments	Playgroup Considerations
Flight Instinct (4-8 months)	Dog's natural instinct to explore new territory is evident. May ignore "come" command & see human chasing them as a game. Teething & chewing behaviors continue.	Playgroups with properly matched playmates. Reward "come"; be sure no negatives or discipline are given when dog comes. Needs to learn "come" is a safe command to follow.
Fear Impact Period 2 (6-14 months)	Fear of change or new experiences. Dependent on growth spurts so dog may go through more than one during period. May be uncomfortable with "unfamiliar" situations & people. Do not force dog into situations.	Playgroups with properly matched playmates. Work to build confidence and do not force into new situations. Use patience & understanding; allow dog to come around on their own.
Maturity (1-4 years)	Timing differs by breed with average being 18 months – 3 years. Smaller breeds mature earlier than larger breeds. Confident dogs may challenge & display aggressive behaviors. Effective management, strong relationships and training is critical to minimize aggression, bites, and territorial displays. Reward "watchdog" behaviors you want & redirect high arousal displays.	Playgroups with properly matched playmates. Effective management and leadership is very important with consistent enforcement of rules. Watch for resource guarding or inappropriate aggressive behaviors. Allow appropriate dog-to dog interactions

Appendix C – Troubleshooting

COMMON PLAYGROUP PROBLEMS & SOLUTIONS

Problem	Proactive Solutions
Event/Activity: Perceived Danger	
Passers-by create high excitement in outdoor play yard	• Privacy fencing or tarp screens placed on lower 6' of open fencing. • Teach "come" to all dogs and use with those who lead the "alarm bark." • Body block the dogs from the area where they perceive the danger.
Passers-by create high excitement in indoor play yard	• Cover lower 6' of windows w/ tinting, paint, or boards. • Teach "come" to all dogs and use with those who lead the "alarm bark." • Body block the dogs from the area where they perceive the danger.
Facility tours create high excitement	• Close-off playrooms from other parts of facility. • Use web cams or video loop of dogs interacting in off-leash play that can be viewed from your entrance or lobby. • Teach "come" to all dogs and use with those who lead the "alarm bark."
Event/Activity: Going for a Walk	
Dog pulls on leash	• Establish rule of "loose leash" walking. • Refer problem dogs to obedience training.
Dog charges through doorways	• Establish rule of "waiting" at doorways. • Practice daily during periods of low excitement or activity in small groups. • Reward success and be consistent during periods of high excitement. • Give dog a timeout for bad behavior.
Event/Activity: Resource Guarding	
Guarding signals & behavior affecting group harmony	• Put dog on NILIF program (see appendix C) • Crate dog during play with toys • Increase number of toys so they exceed number of dogs • Refer dog for behavior modification

Problem	Proactive Solutions
Event/Activity: Reuniting with the group	
Dog arriving for off-leash playgroup creates high excitement	• Build an entry chute into all play areas (4x6 with gates on two sides-not solid so dog can see and smell others). • Establish rules for "self-control" greetings at chute, "wait" at doorways, and "back-up" from chute door & walls. • Crate dogs who get highly aroused and don't self-control during arrival periods. • Crate dogs who are very nervous or insecure during arrival periods. • Shift dogs into an "entry" playgroup that is comprised of dogs with good self-control; then transition to the larger playgroup. • Temporarily house all dogs at arrival in crates/runs and release into playgroup at same time. Start with dogs who exhibit good self-control. Wait for the group to calm prior to adding dogs to the playgroup.
Arriving dog jumps on you when entering play area	• Use body blocks and ignore dog until he exhibits self-control.
Dog gets highly aroused as dogs depart the playgroup.	• Establish rules for "self-control" at chute, "wait" at doorways, and "back-up" from chute door & walls. • Crate dogs who get highly aroused and don't self-control during departure periods. • Crate dogs who are very nervous or insecure during arrival periods. • Temporarily house all dogs at departure times in crates/runs until pick-up.
Event/Activity: Toys & Play	
High excitement	• Remove toys from group • Remove highly aroused dogs for playtimes with toys • Keep play sessions short • Practice obedience during play, e.g., require a "group sit" prior to throwing a ball • Call the dog who is starting to escalate, keep him close until self-control is regained • If using large play area, move to smaller area

Note: Do not force a nervous and insecure dog to obey the "come" command as this puts undue pressure on him. Wait until he gains confidence being in the group before expecting him to come quickly when called.

Nothing In Life is Free (NILIF) Program

This training technique helps establish your role as benevolent leader. It is actually a way of living with your dog that establishes boundaries and rules. Your dog must know basic obedience commands prior to introducing NILIF. See the resource section for good books if you need more information on teaching or using dog obedience commands. These commands are then used to get a behavior you want from the dog before they get what they want. Examples would be the dog must sit and wait for a release before eating a meal or going through the door for a walk.

It is important that rewards and praise be incorporated into the NILIF program. Effective playgroup leaders use obedience training throughout the day in off-leash playgroups.

Working with Confident Dogs

Mature, higher ranking, confident dogs are a great asset in off-leash dog playgroups. They are generally very stable animals who can help maintain stability in a playgroup. But immature, out-of-control, confident dogs are a serious concern. These dogs generally challenge other dogs and people and require extra effort to manage.

Applying some additional "rules" for the challenging dogs may help them defer to your guidance more readily. Consistency is a must as these dogs will look for any opportunity to regain control. These ambitious dogs will notice small shifts in your behavior at any time and will test you.

Following are some tips for reinforcing leadership with these tough cases:

- Determine the top three resources for the specific dog and control these 100% of the time

- List the commands that the dog knows and require one of them prior to allowing him access to any valued resource; be sure to vary the commands
- Set your baseline for acceptable responses (e.g., a 2-second sit) and be consistent; walk away and withhold the resource when the dog's response does not meet your baseline
- Stay cool and calm during all interactions with the dog
- Only pet the dog as a reward for appropriate behaviors or responses to commands
- Body block or ignore demand gestures for petting, play, etc
- Call the dog to you to initiate petting and keep sessions brief
- Keep the dog off any furniture or high places in the play area; if he is in a high place, physically take his space away (e.g., if the dog is lying on a couch, you may sit beside him and physically squeeze him off)
- Don't allow the dog to lie in front of doorways
- Don't allow the dog to lean into you, jump on you or sit in your lap
- Require self-control; praise when you get it and retrain when you don't
- Walk into the dog's space frequently, requiring him to back up or move out or your way. If a dog is lying down, "shuffle" through to get him to move.

Appendix D – Recommended Resources

DOG BEHAVIOR AND BODY LANGUAGE RESOURCES
Books on canine body language, leadership, learning theory, and training. Most of these books and videos are available through Dogwise at http://www.dogwise.com.

- *Calming Signals,* by Turid Rugaas
- *Canine Body Language: A Photographic Guide,* by Brenda Aloff
- *Culture Clash,* by Jean Donaldson
- **Dog Behavior Pamphlets** (especially **Fighting** and **Biting**) by Ian Dunbar
- **Dog Talk DVD,** by Donna Duford
- **Dog-to-Dog Aggression Video,** by Sue Sternberg
- *Dog Language,* by Roger Abrantes
- *Excel-erated Learning,* by Pamela Reid
- *How to be the Leader of the Pack,* by Patricia McConnell
- *How to Speak Dog,* by Stanley Coren
- *The Dog Listener,* by Jan Fennell
- **The Language of Dogs DVD,** by Sarah Kalnjas
- *The Power of Positive Training,* by Pat Miller

DOG DAYCARE RESOURCES
- *How to Own and Operate A Dog Daycare,* by Robin Bennett
- Daycare consulting products and services at http://www.allaboutdogdaycare.com
- Daycare consulting and training programs by Urban Tails Academy at http://www.urbantails.cc
- Daycare lists at Yahoogroups, visit http://groups.yahoo.com/ and search for either dogdaycare or nadda (or both). Join the lists using the information provided.

TRADE ASSOCIATIONS
ABKA - the trade association for pet service providers, http://www.abka.com/

Index

About the Authors

ROBIN BENNETT, CPDT, is the co-owner of All About Dogs, the largest dog training company in Virginia. Since beginning her company in 1993, she has grown from a sole proprietorship to a Corporation that boasts fourteen instructors teaching private lessons as well as numerous group classes and behavior modification lessons for shy, fearful, and aggressive dogs.

Robin has an excellent working relationship with local veterinarians as well as the Prince William Animal Control Bureau. She is recommended by both groups to evaluate potentially dangerous dogs. Robin successfully owned and operated her own dog daycare for many years. Her book, *All About Dog Daycare...A Blueprint for Success,* is the number one reference on owning a daycare, and Robin is a highly sought-after speaker on numerous dog daycare and playgroup topics around the country.

She is an active member of the Association of Pet Dog Trainers (APDT) and the American Boarding Kennel Association (ABKA), and has a B.A. degree from Roanoke College. Robin regularly attends dog-training seminars and has earned Level 1 certification through the Certification Council for Professional Dog Trainers (CCPDT), the first national certification for dog trainers. Robin is a Lieutenant Colonel in the United States Marine Corps Reserve and is married with two children.

Robin's expertise is regularly tapped by the media. Recent press includes a mention in Washingtonian Magazine as one of the best training facilities in the DC area, the Washington Post, the Potomac News, BARK Magazine, Dogs USA Magazine, and Training Secrets for Rottweilers Magazine.

Susan R Briggs, CKO,

is co-owner of Urban Tails, LLC, a dog daycare and full service pet facility in Houston, TX. With her partners Frances Armstrong and Crista Meyer they opened Urban Tails in December 2000 offering the first cage-free sleepovers for large dogs in Houston. A  mission to provide services focused on the health and safety of pets in their care turned to an early passion to promote dog daycare safety.

As active members of ABKA, the trade association for pet service providers, Susan pursued including dog daycare facilities as association members. In 2003, she accepted the position of Dog Daycare chair and worked with a committee of daycare owners from across the country to develop the first facility and operating standards for the dog daycare industry. These standards were published in 2007 as a part of the ABKA's Voluntary Facility Accreditation (VFA) program.

In 2007 Susan was elected to the ABKA board of directors and currently serves as Region 8 director representing members in Arkansas, Louisiana, Oklahoma, and Texas. She also serves on the ABKA VFA committee providing expertise on dog daycare services.

Susan and her partners have presented seminars on dog daycare services at ABKA regional and national conventions. After repeated requests to offer training for others, they started Urban Tails Academy, which offers pet professional training and consulting services. Their courses focus on hands-on technical experience in dog daycare and pet facilities operations.

Susan has a Masters of Accountancy from Truman State University in her home state of Missouri. She has converted into a Texan and lives in Houston with partner, Bill Kamps; three dogs, Hallie, Hank, and Sheppy; and Sydney, her 20-year-old feline.